Dzhomba:
Kalmyk Tea

Nikolai Burlakoff, Editor

To Edward with affection and appreciation Hette,

N. Burlakoff

ÆLITAPRESS.org

AElitaPress.org
12 Charles Place
Ossining, NY 10562
nburlakoff@aelitapress.org

Library of Congress Control Number: 2015902779
CreateSpace Independent Publishing Platform, North Charleston, SC

ISBN: 1505923999
ISBN-13: 978-1505923995

DEDICATION

Dedicated to our mothers: Buga Boskhomdzhievna Aralova, Maria Nikolaevna Balzirova, Bova Khyurmeevnv Bordzhanova, Marilyn Means Copeland, Yalman Bembeevna Khalgaeva, Svetlana Nikolaevna Olefer, Eleanor Griffiths Shaw, Kishtya Boskhomdzhievna Shugraeva

MORNING, WHEN WE DRANK
KALMYK TEA

Through morning windows
The sun warms the table.

I asked the old woman:
Did you know my mother?
Who was she?
Kazanetskaia.
Sveta?
The light-haired one,
Whose locks
On shoulders fell?
Is she alive?
No.

Tears glistened.
The Kalmyk tea got saltier.

And I was glad for that old woman,
Once more, I saw my mother,
That morning we drank tea.

УТРОМ, КОГДА МЫ ПИЛИ
КАЛМЫЦКИЙ ЧАЙ

Утром в окна
Солнце греет стол.

Спросил я старушку:
– А маму Вы знали?
– Кого?
– Казанецкую.
– Светочку?
   Златовласую,
   у которой локоны
   на плечи падали?
   Жива?
– Нет.

И слезы блеснули в глазах.
И более солёным стал калмыцкий чай.

И рад я был старушке,
И снова видел маму,
И утром пили чай.

CONTENTS

Poems

Explanatory Materials

Dzhomba served at annual MACA Chinggis Khan Ceremony,
Princeton Marriott, Princeton, New Jersey, 2014
(Photo N. Burlakoff)

ACKNOWLEDGMENTS

Red Pine, aka Bill Porter, who is probably the foremost current translator of old Chinese poetry and Mahayana sutras, once said in an interview: "American's don't read much poetry, much less Chinese poetry." The same statement is applicable to translations of Russian poetry, and more so to Kalmyk. Few American even know that a people called Kalmyks exist, or that a sizeable community lives in the United States. This short book, therefore, is a testament to a small group of "true believers" who have given much of themselves, not for fame or fortune but to make our shared human story fuller and richer.

The idea of creating a work dedicated to Kalmyk tea, a deeply significant traditional part of Kalmyk culture, belongs to the poet, dramatist, and scholar Rimma Khaninova. It is she who has worked ceaselessly to create an international team of poets, translators, and scholars to make the idea of this book a reality. Erdne Eldyshev and Vera Shugraeva, both recipents of the title: Kalmyk National Poet, are owed a deep debt of gratitude for translation of Russian-language poems into Kalmyk. Tamara Basangova was generous with her article about tea ritual and informal advice and help. Carleton Copeland did his usual first-rate translations of Pushkin, Mihail Khoninov, and Rimma Khaninova's poetry. Elzabair Guchinova was generous in sharing her writing about Kalmyk tea and tea making in the U.S. and in her advice on further research.

It would be remiss not to acknowledge, and express appreciation for, the translations done by V. B. Chongonov, Semon Lipkin, Walter May, and Avril Pyman, among others.

The Mongolian-American Cultural Association and their President, Sanji Altans, and the New Jersey Folk Festival need to be thanked for their financial support.

This work, as all my others, would have been impossible without the constant help and support of my editor and wife, Gail S. Burlakoff.

Moon Motel, Howell, New Jersey, February, 2011
(Photo N. Burlakoff)

INTRODUCTION
Nikolai Burlakoff

> May your bowl of Kalmyk tea
> Never be empty.
> May your journey
> Always be white.
> May you always be
> Welcomed and honored.
> May all beings know
> Only peace and contentment!
>
> *Ioral (poetic well-wish)*

The night of March 4, 2011, I spent in the Moon Motel on Route 9 in Howell, New Jersey. It was a motel that had seen better days, to put it kindly, but I was looking for a cheap price and nearness to Kalmuk Road, where I was to attend the Kalmyk (Western Mongol people from Russia) Spring Holiday—Tsagan Sar. Literally meaning "White Month," it is the holiday celebrating the end of winter and arrival of spring; some in the community view it as the Kalmyk New Year. Traditionally the Kalmyk New Year, and prime holiday, has been Zul, which marks the beginning of winter, but in America Tsagan Sar has become the most important celebration. I spent the night near the Tashi Lhunpo Buddhist temple on Kalmuk Road because services were to be held at 7:00 the next morning, and driving the 80 miles home, after attending the evening services on the 4th, and then back again in the morning seemed excessive.

There were only a handful of us in the temple on that snow-covered and chilled early morning—a sharp contrast to the crowd that had filled it the evening before. As we gathered in the sunrise and warmth of the temple hall we began breaking our fast with a cup of Kalmyk tea (a robust mix of tea, milk, butter, and salt) and a type of unsweetened fry-bread called *bortsoki*. Sara Andreyev, a member of the congregation and a local business and political leader, suggested to me that I talk to an elderly lady sitting at one of the banquet tables. Sara said, "Nick, you should talk to Sonya. She

3

speaks Russian and is one of the original pioneers who came from Yugoslavia in 1951." I thanked Sara, went up to the lady and her companions, introduced myself, and we started speaking Russian. Soon I learned that Sonya grew up in Belgrade, Yugoslavia (today's Serbia). Something prompted me to ask one of those silly questions that locals often ask of a traveler who mentions a town the local has heard of: "Did you, perhaps, know my mother?"

Sonya enquired, "What was her name?" Quickly realizing that she would have no idea of mother's married names I gave the maiden name. "You mean Sveta (using the diminutive for mother's first name—Svetlana)? Is she alive?" Sonya asked. I was thunderstruck! What are the probabilities that two people of different generations, from different ethnic groups, from different countries, meeting in the rural township of Howell, New Jersey, would know a third person after a six decade-long separation? Tears began welling in my eyes, and for a second I imagined that Mother, who had died some two decades earlier, was sitting in front of me. We continued our conversation and then parted. I can still feel the brightness and warmth of the sun from that cold March morning.

For me, the spiritual and emotional genesis of this book springs from that fabulous encounter. I am deeply grateful to Sonya Dzevzinov[1], the lady whose picture graces the cover of this book, and who was a former classmate of my mother's, for bringing Mother back for a split second. It was she who motivated me to dedicate the book to the mothers of the members of the creative team who contributed to it.

***

The instigator of the project, Rimma Khaninova, a poet and professor of literature at Kalmyk State University, suggested a proposal for creating a collection of folkloric texts, poems, expository materials, and images to celebrate the significance of Kalmyk tea. A two-year creative process ensued; as the Russian proverb states, "Quickly the tale is told, but slowly the deed is done."

The process was slow for several reasons. Time was needed not only for proper translations of the artistic and expository materials, but also for finding a way to organize and present the materials in a manner that would resonate with readers of three different cultures and languages. One

---

[1] Sonya's name has also been given to me as Sanja Dzherdzinov.

goal of the project was to present the artistic texts in English, Russian, and Kalmyk. Explanatory materials were limited to English on the theory that they could be found easily in Russian and Kalmyk, but not in English. Time was also needed to discern, comprehend, and find ways to clarify how changes in the technology of communication affected the very nature of the dissemination and interpretation of cultural text. This book does not merely present texts of literary and contextual interest; it includes the very latest in online cultural dissemination, thereby proposing that cultural artifacts and conceptions are in constant evolution and renegotiation as to their role in the life of a contemporary community or communities.

The heart of the book lies in traditional and individually written creative texts. The folkloric texts are of an unknown provenance but are either in current usage or have been recorded as early as the 19th century. Authored texts go as far back as 1829 and in original poetic composition continue to 2008. If one considers the translation of poetic texts as a creative act in its own right, then that process continued for this book to the end of 2014. In addition to the aforementioned texts, and thanks to the almost instantaneous and global reach of contemporary communication directly affecting the theme of this book, important bits of cultural communication were encountered and incorporated, literally, until the book was in galley form, i.e. the preliminary version of the printed book.

Evidence of cultural interconnectedness is illustrated by a personal experience narrative shared on Facebook in the summer of 2014 by Andrey Zobaev, a resident of Elista, Kalmykia. It recounts how eight Kalmyk soldiers from the only Kalmyk settlement in Dagestan were remembered in 1959 by the ninth—the lone Kalmyk survivor from that village. That reminiscence (the one text offered in English only) is added to the more "classical" folkloric texts because it is a contemporary expression of folkloric processes, i.e. informal transmission of traditions.

The very last contribution, which helps delineate the contemporary cultural context for Kalmyk tea, came when the book was in galley form. This was a YouTube video, seen in 2014 but originally distributed in 2012, which demonstrates how to cook Kalmyk tea, adapted to contemporary outdoor preparation in an urban setting. Observations based on that demonstration and the recipe of Kalmyk tea used in the video are in the culinary section of this book. These last two items are an interesting supplement to the conventional gathering of folkloric texts by physical travel to a particular site. They represent today's methods of gathering information that has immediate global distribution and presence.

This book, which is primarily aimed at an English-language reader but is richer for readers of two or more languages, is divided into three major sections: **Folkloric Texts**, **Poems**, and **Explanatory Materials**. Preceding the texts sections is a short segment written by the noted social anthropologist Elzabair Guchinova. Her description of the way Kalmyk tea was prepared in America in the 1990s by Purma Muschajew, a resident of Philadelphia, Pennsylvania, serves as a guide to those who may not be familiar with Kalmyk tea preparation. It will help readers understand various references in the texts to different aspects of tea making. In this instance, as in the balance of the book, extensive passages of translated text are set in a different font to distinguish them.

***

Folkloric Texts include *iorals* (poetic well-wishes)—perhaps one of the most characteristic of Kalmyk folklore genres, as well as legends of origin, proverbs, a riddle, a proverbial saying, and a personal-experience narrative collected on the Internet.

The **Poems** section begins with Alexander Pushkin's *MONUMENT* and *TO A KALMYK MAIDEN*. Although Pushkin's "Monument" does not deal with Kalmyk tea, it is included here, in part, because the translation into Kalmyk was made by Mikhail Khoninov, father of poet Rimma Khaninova, and also because it represents a statement that Russian literature is part of the Kalmyk cultural experience. Next comes the work of two Kalmyk women poets, Bosya Sangadzhieva and Vera Shugraeva, both of whom have written poems titled *KALMYK TEA*. Mikhail Khoninov's poem, titled *ХАЛЬМГ ЦӘ УУДГТАН ҢAPH* in Kalmyk, follows, with two different translations in Russian and one English. The section ends with Rimma Khaninova's series of poems: *TEA BUSH, DZHOMBA, It's Often Said, PUSHKIN'S TEXTS*, and *TEA AND TEA BOWL*. The theme of the poet's role in society, introduced in Pushkin's "Monument," is considered in both Michail Khoninov's and his daughter Rimma's poems. Rimma Khaninova's ending poem asks the question of the fate of Kalmyk tea in the contemporary world, and by extension the fate of the people whose culture is so intertwined with it.

In the **Explanatory Texts** section, the first article, HISTORY AND VIEWS OF KALMYK TEA, gives the history of Kalmyk tea as it is expressed in personal experience. Of great interest are the passages relating the initial reactions to Kalmyk tea by Westerners such as Alexandre Dumas, père— author of *The Three Musketeers* and *Grand Dictionnaire de cuisine* [Big Dictionary of Cookery], among many others books. KALMYK TEA AS RITUAL & CEREMONY, by the noted folklorist of Kalmyk lore, Tamara Basangova, focuses on rituals connected with Kalmyk Buddhism and Kalmyk tea preparation. Her article is particularly interesting when considering some of the contemporary interpretations regarding tea rituals given by Alexandra Burataeva in the KALMYK TEA RECIPES article. Russian and Mongolian cultural contexts elaborate the history of Kalmyk tea in TEA IN RUSSIA, PRESSED TEA, AND "MONGOLIAN" BREWING, and THE *AAGH, PIALA* OR TEA BOWL focuses on the most important implement in tea ceremonies. The issues involved in language and culture translation, particularly translations of poetry, are broached in ON TRANSLATIONS: NOTES AND COMMENTARY. That article also gives contextual data and interpretations of some of the poems so as to enrich the reader's understanding of the poems and their significance in the relationship between tea and culture. Thumbnail sketches of the contributors round out this section of the book.

Every effort has been made to present Kalmyk tea as an item of culture in as wide a context as possible, with as many analytic approaches as came to mind. The functional goals that guided the work from the beginning were to introduce English- and Russian-language speakers to the rich spiritual and gustatory world of Kalmyk tea and to provide materials about this important element of Kalmyk spiritual culture in English, Russian, and Kalmyk. If the book also serves as a seed to motivate Kalmyks to petition UNESCO to recognize *dzhomba* as an intangible heritage item, the two-year trek would have a particularly pleasant flavor. Such a designation would also give an affirmative answer to the question posed by Rimma Khaninova in her poem *TEA AND TEA BOWL*. For those unfamiliar with Kalmyks, the Introduction ends with an historical sketch.

As the book evolved a larger, more overarching goal appeared: the hope that at least some readers will discover here a reality through which they are able to emotionally and in their imagination visit the world of nomad Kalmyks and join in the ritual of partaking of *dzhomba*. One hope is that readers, upon immersion in this book, will be ready to undertake their own journeys into traditions unfamiliar to them. In my own case the poetry and traditions elicited the penning of a light poem about Pushkin and his adventures with Kalmyk tea, initially written in Russian from the point of view of the Kalmyk maiden:

I served the guest our tea—	Я гостя чаем угостила –
Begrudging neither milk nor salt.	Не жаль ни молока, ни соли.
First, made an altar offering,	Сперва бурхана напоила
Then gave the wanderer his fill.	Потом уж, страннику дала.
But in nomad's tent he dreamt of legs	Ему-ж кобылы захотелось
In dimness yearning for mare's flesh.	В кибицком мраке грезит ножки,
As in his nest in Peter's city	Как в питерском своем гнезде
Besmirching conscience, inviting sin.	Марает совесть, к греху водит.
The road is long in our wide steppes,	В степи широкой путь далёк,
Honor preserved with *dombra's* help,	Я домброй честь свою спасла
And passion's flame I did extinguish	И страсти пламя угасила
In the old infidel's heart.	У иноверца старика.

***

Kalmyks are a grouping of people, consisting of Western Mongol clans, who have been living since the middle of the 17th century on Russian territory. After World War II, approximately 500 of them immigrated to the United States, with the vast majority settling in New Jersey around Howell Township. In the span of twenty years after their arrival in the U.S. the Kalmyks, devout Buddhists, built three Buddhist temples in Howell, a temple in Philadelphia, and a monastery in Washington Township, New Jersey. The community and temples attracted a number of Anglo-Americans who were interested in studying the Gelug tradition of Buddhism, headed by the Dalai Lama, and it is not an exaggeration to say that Kalmyks brought the practice of Tibeto-Mongolian Buddhism to America. The journey to Howell began after the Russian revolution and subsequent Civil War, was interrupted for a time by settling in Serbia and other Central and Western Europen countries between the two World Wars, and continued after WWII to the United States.

The Kalmyks traditionally were fully pastoral nomads; they did not make fodder for their herds for the winter and they needed huge tracts of land that could sustain their animals in all seasons of the year. Traditionally sheep, horses, and camels comprised Kalmyk herds, while cattle became significant only in the latter part of the 19th century. Some areas near the Urals, and a huge area between the Volga and Don rivers, north of the

Caspian Sea, served these needs admirably. The herding provided food and shelter;[2] cash and goods were traditionally acquired by trade and warfare. The Russians were happy to have the Kalmyks come in the 17th century onto just-conquered lands and help provide security from a number of Turkic tribes. The Russians had insufficient population to defend this land and Kalmyks, being Buddhist,[3] were unlikely to switch allegiances, and therefore could serve as a reliable border defense. The Kalmyks, in turn, were happy to have a strong ally against the Kazakhs and challengers from other Mongol groupings.

The agreement reached between them was simple in concept: the Kalmyks were allowed to have an independent state (called a *khanate*) and could use the area for their nomadic purposes. In return, they had to acknowledge the suzerainty of the Russian state, swear not to raid Russian settlements for booty, and help the Russians in their conflicts with the Ottomans and various other Muslim ethnic groups.

For a while this arrangement worked well for both sides. The period between 1669 and 1724, the reign of Ayuka Khan, is seen as the golden age of the Kalmyk Khanate. Eventually, for a variety of reasons, the periodically updated agreements fell apart, and in 1771 approximately 75 percent of the Kalmyks left Russia to return to their ancestral lands in Dzhungaria (today's northern half of Xinjiang province in northwestern China). In response, Catherine II, the Great, dissolved the Khanate and began to invite foreign settlers to populate the area previously used by the Khanate.

Most of the remaining Kalmyks continued to pursue their nomadic ways, although land for that, particularly winter pasture, shrank substantially with the influx of farmers. Other Kalmyks became involved in Volga and Caspian caviar fishing, and one group became attached to the Don Cossack host (army). This group, the Buzava, left with the Cossacks after the Russian Civil War, for a time settled in France, Yugoslavia, Bulgaria, Czechoslovakia, and Germany, and became the dominant Kalmyk clan in the post-World War II immigration to the United States. Howell became the epicenter of Kalmyk immigration to the US because Russian Cossacks, who immigrated earlier to this area, assisted their brother Kalmyk Cossacks.

***

---

[2] Wool from sheep was turned into felt that covered the *gers* (yurts) of the nomads.

[3] The neighbors who threatened Russian borders at the time were Muslims.

Mrs. Badushov serving *dzhomba* at the New Jersey Folk Festival,
New Brunswick, New Jersey, 2014
(Photo N. Burlakoff)

MAKING KALMYK TEA IN AMERICA
Elzabair Guchinova

Elzabair Guchinova, a Kalmyk social anthropologist who has written extensively about the 1943-1957 deportation and exile of Kalmyks within the USSR, has, in her book *The Street 'Kalmuk Road'*, which is one of the best and most recent fieldwork studies of the Kalmyk diaspora community in Howell, New Jersey, and Philadelphia, described how Kalmyk tea affected the identity of that group, and how they fared in the United States in the late 1990s:

One cannot leave in silence the fundamental drink of Kalmyks—Kalmyk Tea, which should, more accurately, be described as a liquid food dish. In Kalmykia it is prepared from "brick" tea, except in cases of those who prefer the India manner of tea preparation. Kalmyks who live in Russia, but outside of the border of the Kalmyk Republic, usually request that visitors bring a "brick" of compressed tea, so that they can prepare real Kalmyk Tea—*dzhomba*, at home. That kind of tea [pressed Georgian brick tea] does not exist in the U.S.A., therefore black tea in tea bags is used and without the addition of any aromatic herbs. Lipton is the tea normally used.

In the U.S., Purma Muschajew showed me how she prepares *Dörbet tse* (Dörbet tea). In a three-quart saucepan, she boiled three bags of Lipton tea, which were previously tied together so that they could be pulled out of the pan with one dip of a soup ladle. Afterwards the young woman scooped out the brew one hundred times and then poured it back in into the pot (*samrkh*), eventually adding, in the following order: milk, butter, salt, and nutmeg. The tea with milk was brought to a boil. When the tea was ready, first of all—despite it being evening, she poured into a special silver cup *deedzhin tsogts* a *deedzhi*—the first serving designated for the spirits.

Another woman told me that she completely dislikes the Kalmyk tea as it is prepared in the Kalmyk Republic, regardless who would serve it—too much milk. "So, how do you cook it?" "I throw in the Lipton tea bag, and not yours ("brick" tea of second quality) which is not sorted—some sort of sticks. Then, I add a bay leaf; a bit of nutmeg, salt, and finished off with cream." It's true; in the States brick tea is not popular.

"Sometimes we get brick tea from Russia, as a gift. We have become unused *ter tseekhes* (to that tea)—the taste *taldan* (is different). My family hides the Russian tea from me because, from time to time, when I make tea I'll add some; my people simply can't drink it then."

In its most Americanized form Kalmyk tea is not cooked in a large pot, large enough for the whole family, but individually, in one's own mug. The individualism that is encouraged by the dominant society has been reflected on tea drinking; which from a traditional unhurried family ceremony transformed itself into tea made by each individual just for himself. That kind of tea also gives strength, slackens thirst, but you cannot call it *dzhomba*, anymore.

***

Folkloric Texts

His Excellency and Mrs. Altangerel The Ambassador of Mongolia enjoying *dzhomba*
at NJFF, New Brunswick, New Jersey, 2014
(Photo N. Burlakoff)

IORAL: ZUL TEA POETIC GOOD WISH

Tea, though liquid is the highest offering.
Paper, though thin helps in spiritual growth.
Let us taste the tea and intoxicating vodka
And, without reproach take leave of the departing year
Let fortune in the coming year be good,
Let the future be better than the past ...

ЙОРЯЛ, ПОСВЯЩЕННЫЙ ЧАЮ К ПРАЗДНИКУ ЗУЛ

Чай, хоть и жидок, но подношением считается верховным.
Бумага, хоть тонка, но помощница в росте духовном.
Давайте отведаем чая и водки пьянящей
И проводим без обид год уходящий,
Пусть в наступающем году счастье будет хорошим,
Пусть же Грядущее будет лучше, чем прошлое...

Перевод В. Б. Чонгонова

ЗУЛЫН ЦӘӘД ТӘВДГ ЙӨРӘЛ

Цә шиӊгн болвчн, идәнә дееж,
Цаасн нимгн болвчн, номин көлгн.
Уусн цәәhәсн,
Хар әркәсн амсхгов.
Буур җил hарч,
Ботхн җил ирж,
Авсн өмнкнь хөөткәсн сән болҗ,
Цуhар амулӊ эдлх болтха!

***

Tea, though liquid, by covenant, it
Gives honor to gods and ancestors.
Let it, by spreading its aroma
Transform drink to ambrosia

***

Пусть жидок чай, но по завету — им
Почет Богам и предкам воздадим.
Пусть он, свой аромат распространяя,
В аршан напиток древний превращает!

Перевод В. Б. Чонгонова

***

Цə шиңгн болв чигн, идəнə дееж,
Цə-чигəн элвг-делвг болж,
Улан зандарн асхрж,
Уусн маднд аршан болтха!

***

Oh, Allmerciful!
Let there be much tea and *chigan*!
And let Green and White Tara protect us everywhere!
Let, in accord with out *ioral*,
Tables bend
From varied foods,
And that we all
Enjoy a beautiful life
Coursing with purpose!

***

О, Всемилостивый!
Пусть чай да чигян в изобилии стоят!
А Зеленая и Белая Тары – повсюду нас хранят!
Пусть йорялу нашему согласно,
От пищи разнообразной
Ломятся столы,
И чтобы жизнью прекрасной,
Текущей не напрасно,
Наслаждались все мы!

Перевод В. Б. Чонгонова

***

Нә, хәәрхн!
Цә-чигән элвг-делвг болҗ,
Ноһан, Цаһан Дәркин гегән
Евәҗ, өршәҗ,
Цә-чигән,
Альк нег хот-хоолнь
Ширә дүүрч,
Олн-әмтн амулң эдлтхә!

***

Let tea be steeped, its flavor bloom,
Among all other offerings it reigns!
For all who imbibe it in this world,
Let it be the ambrosia of longevity!
And gods above, showing compassion,
Reward us with invincible good fortune!

***

Пусть чай, настаиваясь, пламенеет,
Средь прочих подношений он – главнее!
Для всех, его вкушающих на свете,
Пусть станет он аршаном долголетья!
А Боги свыше, проявив участье,
Нас наградят несокрушимым счастьем.

Перевод В. Б. Чонгонова

Улан цэ зандрж,
Уухнь дееж болж,
Уусн маднд аршан болж,
Ут нас, бат кишг
Олн Деедс заях болтха!

ABOUT TEA AND SALT
(Legend)

A long time ago there lived two rich men. One lived on the right side of the sun's rising; the other lived on the left side of the sun's rising. One had a growing boy; the other was raising a beautiful daughter. Time came for the children's wedding discussion to commence. The courtship began soon after that. But suddenly the son became sick, and after a short illness he died. He was buried on the mountain slope near the lake. Afterward, the bride also died; they cremated her body and buried the ashes near her fiancé.

Many years have passed since that time. From a tree that grew on the mountain slope, two branches grew. They were cut off and thrown in different directions, far, far away. From those branches other trees grew. Under one tree salt appeared, and from the leaves of the other they began making Kalmyk Tea.

О ЧАЕ И СОЛИ
(Легенда)

Давным-давно жили-были два богача. Один жил с правой стороны восхода солнца, другой жил с левой стороны восхода солнца. У одного рос сын, у другого росла красивая дочь. Настало время им жениться, замуж выходить. Вскоре состоялось сватовство. Но вдруг заболевает сын и после недолгой болезни умирает. Его похоронили на склоне горы, находившейся около озера. После умерла и невеста, ее тело сожгли и пепел захоронили там же, где лежал ее жених.

С тех пор прошло много лет, и на склоне горы выросло дерево, а на нем появились две веточки, их срезали и бросили в разные стороны далеко-далеко. Из веточек выросли деревья. Под одним деревом появилась соль, из листьев другого — стали варить калмыцкий чай.

ТӨРСКНӘ ТУСК ТУУЛЬ
(ЛЕГЕНДА)

Кезәнә бәәж. Хальмгуд Китдд бәәдг цаг. Китдин хаанд нег сәәхн шову беглэд авч ирдг болна. Тер шовун дуулхла, шар нарн теңгрт зогсад, соңсдг бәәж.

— Эн шовунд алтм терм кеһэд, хунын өрүлгэр девскр кеһэд, хаана замас тетктн, — гиж хан түшмүлмүдтэн закв.

Негдгч министран шову хэлэдгт һарһна.

— Шовуг сәәнэр хэлэтн, тегэд эн шовун дуулад, мана чикнэ хужр хаңһах.

Хаана келсиг цугинь күцәнэ.

Өрүн болһн шовуна ду соңсхар хан күлэнэ, болв шовун дуулхш.

— Цевр аһарт сул бәәсн шовун өргэд бүтжэх болна, — гиж хан санад, терминь орчлңгд уга сәәхн садт һарһулна, болв шовун тагчг.

Хан шовуг һазаран һарһулна.

— Ода юнь тату болад эн эс дуулҗахмб? — болна.

Хан түшмүлмүдиннь цецнэснь дуудна, селвг сурна.

Зәрмснь хоолын гем ирж гинэ; наадкснь — хотнь зокҗахш болна; һурвдгчнь — дуулдго шовун бәәж гицхэнэ.

— Күүнэ кииләд һарһсна һар шовунд эс зокҗах болвза, — гиж зу наслсн көгшэ бодна.

Бәрәнд орсн залу авч ирэд, келнэ: «Манд чик селвг өгэд, чнни келсэр шовун дуулхла, бидн чамд эм хәэрлхвидн».

Долан хонгтан уха туҥһаһад: «Алвтан эргэд зуучлтн, тиигхлэ дуулвза», – гинэ.

Хан һурвн җилдэн шовутаһан зуучлна.

Болв шовун тер кевтэн тагчг. Шовун һурниһэд, нүднэсн сувсн болсн нульмсан алдад сууна.

Нег дэкҗ яду шагшг урһмлта, элстэ лааһин амнд күрэд ирнэ. Лааһин үмкэ үнрт цуглрсн то-томҗ уга бөкүн-батхн күүнэ хамр-амар орад, амр өгцхэхш. Хумха сандлын ацт термэн өлгчкэд, харул тэвэд, унтцхадг болна. Өрүн эрт, нарн һарх цагла бийэн ясад суухлань, хаана түшмл хааг серүлнэ. Нарн һархла, ормдан сууһад, шовун эрэхнэр эклэд дуулв. Байрин ду эклэд дуулхлань, ү-түмн шовуд нисҗ ирэд, хамдан дуулв.

– Мана шовун эн һазра бээҗ. Эн төрсн һазрнь, тегэд дуулҗана. Эн алтн термин үүдинь секэд, шовуг тэвтн, – гиҗ тер закв.

ON THE ORIGIN OF KALMYK TEA
(Legend)

Long, long ago, when humanity only began, people did not yet use meat for food even though they raised stock: camels, horses, cows, sheep, goats. They ate dairy foods—butter, cottage cheese, *chigan*, and *bozo*—but they did not know about tea. People lived in great want and they were often hungry.

During that primordial time there lived a lama. He kept thinking how to have everyone be fed and rich, and happy with their life. So, the lama prayed for many days.

On the eleventh day, early in the morning, a woman named Tsagan came visiting. The lama interrupted his prayer and greeted her:

"Hello, Tsagan!"

"Hello."

"What's happening in the world? What do you hear?" he asked.

"Nothing," the woman answered. She stood for a while, and then she left.

The lama continued his prayer, and for another ten days he prayed without stopping. Early in the morning of the twenty-first day another woman appeared to him. The lama interrupted his prayer and greeted the woman:

"Hello, Sangadzhi!"

"Hello."

"What's new and interesting in the world that you hear?"

"Nothing, everything is as it always has been," answered Sangadzhi, and after standing for a while, she left.

The lama became thoughtful: "How is it that I am praying for twenty days now without sleep and rest, and it is all for nothing?"

Nevertheless, he stoically continued to pray for another ten days. On the thirty-first day, in the morning, when the sun had barely risen, a twelve-year-old boy appeared to him, a novice. The lama interrupted his prayer and greeted him.

"Hello, novice!"

"Hello."

"What have you seen? What have you heard?"

"Oh," the boy exclaimed, "from the side of the sunrise the steppe is completely covered with unusual plants with red, yellow, and blue flowers. It's pleasant to look at; it became so beautiful!

The lama became happy

"You have a golden tongue! May you be fortunate, boy, and live long."

The lama finished his prayer by delivering a beautiful blessing.

Some time passed. When the flowers began to fall off the people gathered to discuss the strange plants that appeared on the steppe, and what use there could be from them. Whoever had something—a knife, a hatchet—would cut off the leaves and dry them. Someone had the idea to throw a handful of these leaves into boiling water, adding some milk, salt, and butter. That is how Kalmyk tea came into being, and we drink it to this day.

О ПРОИСХОЖДЕНИИ КАЛМЫЦКОГО ЧАЯ
(Легенда)

Давным-давно, когда человечество только зарождалось, люди еще не употребляли в пищу мяса, хотя разводили скот: верблюдов, лошадей, коров, овец, коз. Питались они молочными продуктами — маслом, творогом, чигяном, бозо, но чая не знали. Люди жили в острой нужде и часто оставались голодными.

В то же изначальное время жил один лама. Он размышлял над тем, как сделать всех сытыми и богатыми, довольными своей жизнью. И лама в течение многих дней читал молитву.

На одиннадцатый день, ранним утром, к нему зашла женщина по имени Цаган. Лама прервал молитву и поприветствовал ее:

– Здравствуй, Цаган!

– Здравствуйте.

– Что там происходит в мире, что слышно? – спросил он.

– Ничего, – ответила женщина, постояла немного и ушла.

Лама продолжил свою молитву и еще в течение десяти дней он беспрерывно молился. Ранним утром двадцать первого дня явилась к нему другая женщина. Лама прервал чтение молитвы, поприветствовав женщину:

– Здравствуй, Сангаджи!

– Здравствуйте.

– Что нового и интересного слышно в мире?

– Ничего, все по-старому, – ответила Сангаджи и, постояв, ушла.

Лама задумался: «Что же это такое, я уже молюсь двадцать дней без сна и отдыха, а все без толку».

И тем не менее он упорно продолжал молиться еще в течение десяти дней. На тридцать первый день, поутру, едва взошло солнце, явился к нему двенадцатилетний мальчик Манджи. Лама прервал молитву и поприветствовал его:

– Здравствуй, Манджи!

– Здравствуйте.

– Что ты видел, что слышал?

– О, – воскликнул мальчик, – со стороны восхода солнца степь сплошь покрылась диковинными растениями с красными, желтыми, синими цветами. Смотреть приятно – так красиво стало!

Лама обрадовался:

– Уста твои золотые! Будь же, мальчик, счастлив и живи долго!

Лама завершил молитву, произнеся красивое благопожелание.

Прошло некоторое время. Когда цветы стали осыпаться, люди собрались обсудить, что это за странные растения появились в степи и какая от них может быть польза. Кто чем – ножом, топором – срезали листья с растений и засушивали их. Кто-то догадался бросить щепотку этих листьев в кипящую воду, добавил молока, соли, масла. Так появился калмыцкий чай, который мы пьем и доныне.

Чигян – коровье заквашенное молоко.

Бозо – гуща, остающаяся после перегонки молочной калмыцкой водки.

ХАЛЬМГ ЦӘӘҺИН ТУСК ТУУҖ
(ЛЕГЕНДА)

Кезәнә, әмтн үүдәд, төрәд һарсн цагла цуһарн үсн, чигән, тосн, аарц, боз ууһад, идәд тежәлән авдг бәәж. Темә өскәһәд, мөр өскәһәд, үкр өскәһәд, хө өскәһәд, яма өскәһәд йовдг бәәж. Мах гидг йом дуусн иддго бәәж. Әмтн түрү, өлн бәәж.

Нег цагин аңхунд лам күн бәәж. Эн лам ухалад, әмтиг дүүрн, цатхлн, ханлһта бәәдгинь хәәһәд, хальмг һазрт цә урһахар номд орв. Арвн хонгтан сууһад, өдр-сө уга ном давтад суув.

Арвн хонг сууксн цагла, өрүн өрүһәр нег Цаһан гидг нертә гергн орж ирв. Лам номан төгсәһәд, «Менд, Цаһаң», – гижәнә. – «Менд». «Цаачн юн үзгднә, юн соңгсгдна?» «Юмн угал», – гинә. Тиигәд келәд зогсчаһад, одак гергн һарад йовж одв. Ламин зергәс дәкәд арвн хонгар номан давтад орв. Арвн хонгтан сууһад ном кеһәд бәәв. Дәкәд нег өрүн номин цег деер гергн күн орж ирв. Номан зоһсхаһад лам сурж бәәнә: «Менд, Саңгдж». – «Менд». «Цаачн юн үзгднә, юн соңгсгдна?» – «Юн үзгдхм, юн соңгсгдхмн, юмн уга», – гиж келәд, зогсчаһад, гергн һарад йовад одв. Лам уха гүүлгәһәд ухалад, санҗана: «Мууха юмб, угад оршн гижәхмби, би ода хөрн хонгтан ном кеһәд, давталд суучкув», – гинәд санад, дәкәд арвн хонгар номин давталд орв. Арвн хонгтан сууһад окв. Бас нег өрүн нарн һарсна хөөннь арвн хойрта Манҗ орж иржәнә.

Ламин зергәс номан төгскәhәд: «Манҗ, мендүвтә», – гижәнә. «Менд». – «Ю соңгсуч, ю үзүч?» – «О, – гижәнә Манҗ, – эн нарн hарх үзг, эн ташу кевтән ху цецгә болҗ одв: улан, шар, көк, цецгә урhад бәәҗ. Хәләхлә – дегд сәәхн». Лам: «Амнчн яhсн сәәхн юмб, ут нас, бат кишг эдлх бол», – гиhәд зәрлг болҗана. Манҗ hарад йовад одв. Ламин зергәс арднь номан аальдад төгскәhәд сәәхн йөрәл тальвад төгскв.

Тиигәд кесг хонад, цецгә хатад унад, әмтн хамг цуглрад, «Эн юн гидг юмн hазрас урhсн болхв эн?» – гиhәд, утхарн тәәрәд, сүктәнь сүкәрн тәәрәд авч ирәд, хатсаhад, ус буслhаhад, уснд одак цәәhән тәвәд, терньбудг болад, үслад, тослад, хальмг әмтн тас ууhад, идәд, тиигәд дүүрңг, цатхлн ханлта болад бәәhәд бәәҗ. Хальмгин номин йоснд келгдәг, тууҗд, үлгүр – юуhинь келхлә, цә гидг юмн hазрас ламин күчәр, номин күчәр урhсн гиhәд келдг.

ZUL[4]: ZONKAVA AND TEA
(Legend)

At one time, long ago there lived a wise person named Zonkava,[5] who for many years suffered from a grave illness.

Finally, Zonkava called a well-known doctor. The doctor examined him and said: "A heavenly beverage will help you become cured of your illness."

"What kind of beverage?"

"It is a tea made with milk and salt, it is strong and aromatic. Drink it for breakfast each day, for seven days.

Zonkava began to cook and drink this tea, and his health began to improve. He kept improving and improving, and finally the day arrived when the illness left him completely. This happened on the 25th of the first month of winter, according to the lunar calendar. He arose from his bed, went out into the fresh air, and could not get his fill of the beautiful day, and his miraculous recovery from a deadly illness.

From that day on, at Zonkava's command, the Kalmyks celebrate each 25th day of the first winter month the holiday of Zul. On that day, every Kalmyk, from the smallest to the biggest, adds one year to their age. On that day, in honor of deities, vigil lights (*zul*) are lighted, and the tea ritual is conducted as an offering.

---

[4] Zul: 1) New Year's holiday; 2) votive light
[5] Zonkava: Tsongkapa founder of the Gelug Buddhist school

The celestial beverage was called from that time onward, Kalmyk tea or dzhomba[6], and has been regarded as the first dish. Elders, while drinking tea during the Zul festival, speak the following benediction:

> Annually celebrating
> Zul and Tsgan Sar[7],
> Imbibing noble
> Zonkava's nectar,
> Taking our proper
> Place among
> The six kinds of sentient beings[8],
> Let us live for one hundred years!

Among the people, from that time onward, the following proverb became popular: Tea, though liquid, is the head of all dishes; paper, though thin, is the servant of science and learning.

---

[6] *Dzhomba*: best kind of Kalmyk tea
[7] Tsagan Sar: lit. "White Month," holiday marking beginning of spring.
[8] Six classes, or kinds, of beings: 1) *naraka*-hell beings; 2) *preta*-hungry ghosts; 3) *tiryak*-animals; 4) *manusya*-humans; 5) *asura*-evil spirits; 6) *deva*-divine beings.

ЗУЛ[9]
(Легенда)

Когда-то очень давно жил мудрый человек по имени Зункава, который много лет страдал тяжким недугом. Однажды Зункава обратился к одному известному лекарю. Тот, осмотрев его, сказал:

– Вам поможет излечиться от этой болезни божественный напиток.

– Что же за напиток?

– Это чай с молоком и солью, крепкий и ароматный. Пейте его на голодный желудок в течение семи дней.

Зункава стал варить и пить такой чай, и здоровье его пошло на поправку. Ему становилось все лучше и лучше, и, наконец, настал тот день, когда болезнь окончательно покинула его. Это было 25-го числа первого зимнего месяца по лунному календарю. Зункава поднялся с постели, вышел на свежий воздух и не мог нарадоваться на белый свет, на свое чудесное исцеление от смертельного недуга.

С тех пор, по велению Зункавы, калмыки каждый день 25-го числа первого зимнего месяца отмечают праздник Зул. В этот день все калмыки от мала до велика прибавляют к своему возрасту по одному году. В честь бурханов в этот день возжигают лампадки (зул) и совершают чайный ритуал подношения. Божественный напиток, ниспосланный калмыкам, стал называться с тех пор калмыцким чаем или джомбой и считается первым угощением.

---

[9] 1) Праздник первого месяца зимы 2) лампада

Старцы, когда пьют чай в праздник Зул, произносят такое благопожелание:

> — Справляя ежегодно
> Зул и Цаган Сар[10],
> Вкушая благородный
> Зункавы нектар,
> Занимая место
> Достойное в среде
> Шести видов жизни[11],
> Да проживем сто лет!

С того времени в народе популярна поговорка: чай, хоть и жидкий, – глава всех блюд, бумага, хоть и тонкая, – слуга науки и ученья.

---

[10] Цаган Сар – праздник наступления весны (буквально «белый месяц»).
[11] Шесть видов жизни – т.е. шесть видов живых существ.

ЗУЛ
(ЛЕГЕНДА)

Ики кезәнә Зуңква гидг нег гүн номта күн олн җилд күнд хуучта бәәсн бәәҗ.

Зуңква, тегәд тер шалтган нег медрлтә күүнд одад үзүлхләнь тернь: «Тана эн хуучндтн деедсин идән тусан күргх», – гиҗ келнә.

«Не, тер деедсин идән гидгтн юн гидг юмб?» – гиҗ Зуңква тер күүнәс сурна. – «Деедсин идән гисн улан зандн хальмг цә болдм», – гинә.

Тиигәд, Зуңква тер күүнә заасн улан хальмг цәег кесгтән зоогла бәәҗ, бийнь сән болад, шалтгнь эдгәд, зул сарин хөрн тавнд босад, һаза һарад, нарт делкә үзсн болдмн.

Тер өдрәс авн, үкүд шалтгасн тоньлсндан икәр байрлад, эн зул сарин хөрн тавн өдр ик-баһ уга күн болһн нежәһәд нас зүүтхә гиҗ Зуңква зәрлг болсмн.
Тер учр деерәс, хальмгин көгшдүд зулин цә уухларн иим йөрәл тәвдг болсмн:

Җил, өөн хаңцҗ,
Җил болһн
Зул, Цаһаһан кеҗ,
Зуңкван аршанд күртҗ,
Зурһан зүүл хамг әмтнә хормад багтҗ,
Зу наслцхай!

Тер цагас нааран хальмг олн әмтн заагт иим үлгүр һарсн болдг:

Цә шиңн болвчн
Идәни дееҗ болдг;
Цаасн нимгн болвчн
Номин көлгн болдг.

33

PROVERBS

***

No matter how thin the tea—it's served first,
No matter how thin a page—it makes a book.

Как ни жидок чай – первое угощение,
Как ни тонка бумага – основа книги.

Цэ шиӊгн болв чигн хотын дееж,
Цаасн нимгн болв чигн көлгн болдг.

***

No matter how thin the tea—it begins the meal,
No matter how thin the page—it makes a book.

Как ни жидок чай – начало еды,
Как ни тонка бумага – основа книги.

Цэ шиӊгн болв чигн хотын дееж,
Цаасн нимгн болв чигн номин девскр.

***

The more you mix the tea,
The thicker it gets.

Чем больше перемешиваешь чай,
Тем он становится гуще.

Цэ самрх дутман зандрдг.

RIDDLE

***

Dried leaves and stems on top,
Abundant black, springing from the bottom,
Nourishing white, adding flavor,
Fat yellow, ensuring satisfaction.
(Tea, water, milk, salt, butter)

Сушеные листья и стебли, прибывшие сверху,
Обильное черное, прибывшее снизу,
Питательное белое, придающее цвет,
Любимое белое, придающее вкус,
Жирное желтое, заботящееся об удовольствии.
(Чай, вода, молоко, соль, масло).

Деерәс ирсн дерсн-хурсн,
Дорас ирсн элвг хар,
Өңгинь ясдг өл буурл,
Амтинь ясдг амр цаһан,
Тавинь хәәдг тарһн шар.
(Цә, усн, үсн, давсн, тосн).

PROVERBIAL SAYING

FOUR WEAKNESSES

Weak is a tea without salt.
Weak is a youth without a guide,
Weak a stallion without a bridle
Weak is a rope without a twist.

ЧЕТЫРЕ СЛАБЫХ

Слаб чай без соли,
Слаб мальчик без воспитания,
Слаб конь без узды,
Слаба веревка без сучения.

ДӨРВН СУЛ

Давсн уга цә сул,
Сурhл уга көвүн сул,
Хазар уга мөрн сул,
Эрчм уга деесн сул.

ANDREY ZOBAEV'S PERSONAL EXPERIENCE NARRATIVE

... on a cold November morning, near the last house in the village of New Sickle, of the Babayurtovsk District, a middle-aged man appeared. He stood and cried by his house—the one he was born in, and from which he departed for the front lines. He cried and remembered all his relations, and those close to them: those who went to the front lines and never returned those who died from hunger and cold in Siberia.[12] The house owner, a Nogay[13] woman, went from inside the house into the yard. Seeing the man, recognizing him, she began to wipe her tears and lamented:

"Sonny, you're alive, you returned! Allah be praised!'

"Hello, auntie Razyat, I came for a day. No one will return here. Out of the nine Kalmyks who went to the front lines, I am the only one returned. Out of those who were exiled to Siberia more than half did not return, they died. If you would like to help, sell me a sheep and I will commemorate my countrymen."

"Oh, sonny, we'll slaughter the sheep ourselves, and cook the meat and Kalmyk tea, and you can, according to the customs of your forebears, memorialize them yourself," Razyat continued to lament and cry.

By dinnertime all was ready; the Nogay women cooked the meat in one kettle and in the other, Kalmyk tea. The man placed the meat in one pot and poured the tea into another and went in the direction of the abandoned Kalmyk cemetery. He prayed for a long time, as he was taught in his childhood by his grandmother. Having remembered everyone, he returned to the settlement where, together with the Nogays, they remembered and commemorated all Kalmyks.

---

[12] The Kalmyks were internally exiled between 1943 and 1956 to Siberia and Central Asian areas.

[13] A Turkic-speaking people primarily living in the Republic of Dagestan, Russia. Unlike the Kalmyks, who are Buddhist, the Nogay are Muslim.

In the morning he returned from Dagestan, home to Kalmykia after a jurney made in order to preserve the memory of his countrymen and the good neighborly relations of the welcoming Nogay people.

POEMS

"Alexander Pushkin," Rimma Khaninova

A MONUMENT I'VE RAISED NOT BUILT WITH HANDS...
A.S. Pushkin

Exegi Monumentum

A monument I've raised not built with hands,
And common folk shall keep the path well trodden
To where it unsubdued and towering stands
   Higher than Alexander's Column.

I shall not wholly die—for in my sacred lyre
My spirit shall outlive my dust's corruption -
And honour shall I have, so long the glorious fire
   Of poesy flames on one single scutcheon.

Rumour of me shall then my whole vast country fill,
In every tongue she owns my name she'll speak.
Proud Slave's posterity, Finn, and—unlettered still—
   The Tungus, and the steppe-loving Kalmyk.

And long the people yet will honour me
Because my lyre was tuned to loving-kindness
And, in a cruel Age, I sang of Liberty
   And mercy begged of Justice in her blindness.

Indifferent alike to praise or blame
Give heed, O Muse, but to the voice Divine
Fearing not injury, nor seeking fame,
   Nor casting pearls to swine.

Translated by Avril Pyman

41

А.С. Пушкин
***

Exegi monumentum[14]

Я памятник себе воздвиг нерукотворный,
К нему не зарастет народная тропа,
Вознесся выше он главою непокорной
    Александрийского столпа.

Нет, весь я не умру — душа в заветнойлире
Мой прах переживет и тленья убежит —
И славен буду я, доколь в подлунном мире
    Жив будет хоть один пиит.

Слух обо мне пройдет по всей Руси великой,
И назовет меня всяк сущий в ней язык,
И гордый внук славян, и финн, и ныне дикой
    Тунгус, и друг степей калмык.

И долго буду тем любезен я народу,
Что чувства добрые я лирой пробуждал,
Что в мой жестокий век восславил я Свободу
    И милость к падшим призывал.

Веленью божию, о муза, будь послушна,
Обиды не страшась, не требуя венца,
Хвалу и клевету приемли равнодушно
    И не оспоривай глупца.
1836

---

[14]Я воздвиг памятник (лат.)

Александр Пушкин
***

Exegi monumentum

Би һарар эс делдсн
Бумб бийдəн босхув.
Түүнүр əмтнə хаалһ
Тас билрхн уга.
Дарг өгдго ораһарн тер
Александрийск столпаһас давҗ үлв.

Уга, би үкшгов –
Əмм хəəртə частртм,
Үксн цогцм өгрдг болвчн
Уданд би нерəн келүлхүв.
Сар дорк делкəд
Һанцхн шүлгч үлдтл,
Сəəхн туурмҗар җирһхүв.

Алдр цуг Əрəсəһəр
Мини тускар келх,
Аль-бис келнь
Нерим дуудҗ амлх,
Бахта славяна ач,
Финн, эндр зерлг
Бəəх тунгус болн
Теегин иньг – хальмг.

43

Ээлән әмтнд күргҗ
Удан би бәәхүв,
Сән седклин серл
Серүлҗ шүлгәрн дуудлав.
Эврәннь догшн цагла
Сулдхвр би магтлав,
Седклән үрүдснднь өршәлһ
Хәәрлхинь би некләв.

О, үүдәвр минь, бурхни
Евәләр соңсурч бол.
Ө-һундлас әәлго,
Титм бийдән неклго,
Магтал хов хойриг
Кергт бәрлго йович,
Хоосн һәрглә төрүц
Бичә марһич.

Орчулснь Хоньна Михаил

44

TO A KALMYK MAIDEN
A.S. Pushkin

Farewell then, gracious Kalmyk maid!
Though it was never my intent,
I'll have you know I all but stayed,
And, true to form, I nearly went
Across the steppes behind your tent.
Your eyes are slanted, I confess,
Your nose is flat and forehead wide.
You never prattle French or press
Your legs in with a silky glide
Or slice bread by the samovar
In pretty patterns *à l'anglaise.*
You never rave about *Cinq-Mars*[15]
Or fancy Shakespeare overpraised.
You don't fall into reverie
Whenever your sweet head is empty,
Delight in warbling "Ma dov'è,"[16]
Or gallopade in the Assembly.[17]
What matter? For the half an hour
It took before my team could ride,
What occupied my heart and mind
Was your regard and wild allure.
My friends, is it so different
If, dallying, the soul reposes
In splendid halls, exclusive loges,
Or tarries in a nomad's tent?

Translated by Carleton Copeland

---

[15] A historical novel published in 1826 by Alfred de Vigny (1797-1863).

[16] An aria from the opera *Didone Abbandonata* by Baldassare Galuppi (1706-1785).

[17] The Moscow Noble Assembly, a club for the nobility where Pushkin attended balls and undoubtedly danced the gallopade.

А.С. Пушкин
КАЛМЫЧКЕ

Прощай, любезная калмычка!
Чуть-чуть, назло моих затей,
Меня похвальная привычка
Не увлекла среди степей
Вслед за кибиткою твоей.
Твои глаза, конечно, узки,
И плосок нос, и лоб широк,
Ты не лепечешь по-французски,
Ты шелком не сжимаешь ног,
По-английски пред самоваром
Узором хлеба не крошишь,
Не восхищаешься Сен-Маром[1],
Слегка Шекспира не ценишь,
Не погружаешься в мечтанье,
Когда нет мысли в голове,
Не распеваешь: Ma dov'è[2],
Галоп не прыгаешь в собранье…
Что нужды? — Ровно полчаса,
Пока коней мне запрягали,
Мне ум и сердце занимали
Твой взор и дикая краса.
Друзья! Не все ль одно и то же:
Забыться праздною душой
В блестящей зале, в модной ложе
Или в кибитке кочевой?
1829

Александр Пушкин
ХАЛЬМГ КҮҮКНД

Һольшг күүкн, менд үлд!
Генәртә сәәхн авъясм чини
Геринчн ардас намаг дахулад,
Күцсн керггм харш болад,
Көтләд, теегәр йовулн алдв.
Хойр нүдичн лавта бүргр,
Хамрчн хамшһр, маңначн өргн,
Кевшҗ парнцсар чи келхшч,
Кеершҗ, көлән торһар бүтәхшч,
Самоварин өмн англин бәрцәр
Салһҗ, нимгәр өдмг утлхшч,
Сен-Мариг дегд буульҗ,
Шекспириг әрвҗго медсәр магтхшч,
Толһад үүл уга цагла
Тоолад айстан уха туңһахшч,
Наадад Ма-до-ве дуулхшч,
Нәәрин сүүрт биилҗ өсрхшч…
Ямр төрв? Өрәл част,
Ядсн мөрд нанд тачатл,
Соньн хәләцчн, эмнг көркхнчн,
Седкл, зүрким дегц авлв.
Үүрмүд! Седкл амр-таварн
Үзмҗтә өргн ширәд, луңцүлий,
Теегт хальмг герт, санаһан
Тевчҗ аадрулсн эс әдлий?

Орчулснь Көглтин Дава

"Dzomba," Dmitry Sandzhiev

KALMYK TEA
Bosya Sangadzhieva

to L.S. Sobolev

Which Kalmyk was it, out of all the centuries,
Invented that which now I praise to you?
Each day at dawn, arising and remembering,
A cup of golden beverage I brew.

Not warm, nor cold, but gold! With pepper steaming,
With butter and with milk filled to the brink.
And we rejoice at heart, with all our being,
When liberally our Kalmyk tea we drink.

If evening snowstorms howl around your shelter,
Or if the midday heat the grasses grips,
There's not for man a better friend or helper
Than Kalmyk tea, the brew of native steppes.

I recently served a guest with this restorer—
He came to us from very distant parts.
He drank the tea, and then he said: "How glorious!
Here is the real hot steppe-wind's warmth of heart.

I catch in this the summer steppeland's fragrance,
A breath of honeyed rose it brings to mind.
With you first time I make this tea's acquaintance,
A better drink than this I'll never find!"

With great delight I heard the words thus spoken,
And what reply to them was left for me?
And so, his empty cup then having taken,
I filled it up again with Kalmyk tea.

And here the reader's voice is raised in query:
"What does it taste like?" So I answer true:
"Its taste depends upon who brews it, clearly.
So I myself will brew a cup for you!

So please drop in! I'll bring you tea, good fellows,
And friendship too… A small folk we remain.
How will you find us?... We are steppeland dwellers.
Remember Pushkin's 'Kalmyk of the plain'?"

Translated Walter May

Бося Сангаджиева
КАЛМЫЦКИЙ ЧАЙ

Л.С. Соболеву

Какой калмык в какое из столетий
Придумал то, что я воспеть хочу?
Я каждый день, вставая на рассвете,
Напиток золотистый кипячу.

Да не простой, а золотой! Он с перцем,
И с маслом, и со свежим молоком.
Мы счастливы всем существом, всем сердцем,
Когда привольно чай калмыцкий пьем.

Завоет ли вечеровая вьюга,
Придавит ли траву полдневный зной —
Нет лучшего помощника и друга,
Чем наш калмыцкий чай в степи родной.

Я потчевала гостя им недавно,
А гость приехал к нам издалека.
Он пил и приговаривал: «Как славно,
Есть в чае жар сердечный степняка.

В нем запахи я чувствую степные
И чувствую дыханье роз в меду.
У вас его отведал я впервые
И лучшего напитка не найду!»

Приятно было слушать это слово.
Что я могла в ответ ему сказать?
И, чашку взяв у гостя дорогого,
Я чаю налила ему опять.

Но тут читатель голос свой возвысит:
«А вкус его каков?» Я говорю:
От той, кто сварит, вкус его зависит,
И я сама для вас его сварю.

Так приезжайте – угощу вас чаем
И дружбою… Народ наш невелик.
Как нас найти? В степи мы обитаем.
Иль вам напомнить? «Друг степей калмык…»

Перевод Семена Липкина

Сангҗин Бося
ХАЛЬМГ ЦӘ
Л. С. Соболевд

Кезә, кенә хальмг
Келхд, үүдәсинь медхшив,
Зуг өрүн болһн
Зандрсн цәәһән буслһнав.

Цәм эгл биш,
Давста, үстә, тоста,
Таварн сууһад уухла –
Танд юуһинь келхв!

Асхни шуурһн дөгәд,
Агсмнад халун шатвчн,
Төрскн теегтм цәәһәсм
Түшәтә нөкднь уга.

Шидрхн хәрәс ирсн
Шин таньл гиичдән
Хотыннь деежән бәрүлҗ
Хальмг цәәһән нерәдүв.

Гиич цәәһим амсчкад
Герл чирәднь ивтрҗ
Теегин күүнә седклин –
Догшн халун бууҗ.

.

Бал цецгэн үнр
Бас иигҗ ивтрнə.
Теегинтн каңкнсн үнр
Цə дотртн шиңгрҗ,

Күн болҗ урлдан
Күргҗ цəəһитн уужанав,
Энүнəс даву ундн
Олдхинь медхшив! – гив.

Яһсн байрта гиичв!
Ямаран хəрү өгхв?
Дахулн сулдсн ааһднь
Дəкнəс цəəһəсн кевв.

Болв, мини умшач
Бас амтынь соньмсх,
Чансн эзинь медх,
Цəəһин амт күлəх.

Ирсн цагттн танд
Эврəн чанад өгнəв,
Иртн, цəəһəрн тоонав,
Үүрмүд болҗ садлнав.

Маниг олхд амр.
Мөңк теегтəн бəəдвидн.
Танд хайган илгəнəв:
– Теегин иньг – Хальмг!

KALMYK TEA
Vera Shugraeva

Hot tea with nutmeg taste
To honored guests is served:
Imbibe, drink up! It tastes so good,
Our Kalmyk tea—contains all life!

With wooden ancestral cup
We bless the heir,
With altar food of strong
Kalmyk tea—to always be with him.
Imbibe, drink up! It tastes so good,
Our Kalmyk tea—contains all life!

Before the journey's start
A blessing as of old we utter:
Imbibe, drink up—to health!
And, Kalmyk tea we thank!

Translated by Nikolai Burlakoff

Вера Шуграева
КАЛМЫЦКИЙ ЧАЙ

Горячий чай с мускатным вкусом
Гостям почетным поднесем:
– Вкушайте, пейте! Он так вкусен,
Калмыцкий чай – вся жизнь в нем!

Мы деревянной чашей предков
Наследника благословим –
Едой бурханам, чтобы крепок
Был чай калмыцкий всюду с ним.
– Вкушайте, пейте! Он так вкусен,
Калмыцкий чай – вся жизнь в нем!

И перед дальнею дорогой
Йорял[18], как встарь, мы говорим:
– Вкушайте, пейте на здоровье!
Калмыцкий чай благодарим!

Перевела Римма Ханинова

---

[18]Йорял (калм.) – жанр благопожелания.

Шутран Вера
ХАЛЬМГ ЦӘ

Хальмг уурта зандын цәәг
Хәәртә гиичдән бәрүләд өгий:
– Уутн, эдлтн
Цә! Хальмг цә!
    Цә! Хальмг цә!

Хальмг уурта зандын цәәг
Хәәртә гиичдән бәрүләд өгий:
– Уутн, эдлтн
Цә! Хальмг цә!
    Цә! Хальмг цә!

Далһа моднааһар дүүргэд
Деежинь отхн көвүндән нерәдий:
– Уутн, эдлтн
Цә! Хальмг цә!
Цә! Хальмг цә!

Хол хаалһд йовхиннь өмн
Хальмг цәәһәр йөрәл тәвий:
– Уутн, эдлтн
Цә! Хальмг цә!
    Цә! Хальмг цә

Days of Kalmyk Literature, 1973 (l-r): V. Shugraeva, M. Khoninov, A. Balakaev, K. Erendzhenov

WHY THE SUN IS RED
Mikhail Khoninov

Early in the morning
The sun will depart on its journey—
And comes to my window,
And looks attentively.
I ask it to pop in.
It replies:
"I'll come later, I promise …"

"It kept its promise."
It likes to drink tea.
Tea with salt; Kalmyk tea
I indulge the sun.
"Drink up, no need to stint, the pot is full!"
Our faces are redder than sandalwood.

It thanks me, and then,
Having rested,
Slowly-slowly rises,
And walks on the rooftops.
But the house does not splinter,
The house stands illuminated by the languid sun.

The sun welcomes all,
Not hiding light,
As friends,
It welcomes all with a bright smile.
Why is it red, I think?
"It drinks Kalmyk tea, that's why it's red …"

Translated by Nikolai Burlakoff

Михаил Хонинов
ОТЧЕГО СОЛНЦЕ КРАСНОЕ

Ранним утром
Отправится солнышко в путь –
И подходит к окошку
И смотрит внимательно.
Я его приглашаю ко мне заглянуть.
Отвечает:
– Попозже зайду обязательно…

И зашло.
Почаевничать любит оно.
Чаем с солью, калмыцким,
Я солнышко балую.
– Пей, не жалко ведь, чая в кастрюле полно!
Наши лица красней древесины сандаловой.

Мне спасибо оно говорит, а потом,
Отдохнув,
Поднимается медленно-медленно
И по крыше идет,
Но не рушится дом,
Дом стоит озарен светом солнышка медного.

Всех приветствует солнышко,
Свет не тая,
Как друзей,
Всех встречает улыбкою ясною.
Почему оно красное, думаю я?
– Пьет калмыцкий чаек, потому ведь и красное…

Перевел Николай Кутов

THE SUN, DRINKING KALMYK TEA
Mikhail Khoninov

On a clear morning before the long journey
The bending sun peers into my window,
I invite it to the door,
But it responds, simply: "Later."

… Old sol came to drink Kalmyk tea
And it shines before me:
One pot was not enough for us,
We're tamarisk red by the fire.
And in a good mood,
Having rested, appreciatively, it resumes its trek
Of arising—buildings
Bend their shoulders a bit.

The sun gently welcomes everyone on earth.
And I, in childhood, did not know that it
Drank Kalmyk tea and greeted
The Oirat, for a long while, with its red color.

Translated by Nikolai Burlakoff

Михаил Хонинов
СОЛНЦЕ, ПЬЮЩЕЕ КАЛМЫЦКИЙ ЧАЙ

Ясным утром пред дальней дорогой
Солнце смотрит в окно, наклонясь.
Я его приглашаю к порогу,
Говорит, что поздней, не чинясь.

…Чай калмыцкий пришло пить светило
И сияет напротив меня:
Маловато кастрюли нам было,
Тамариском красны у огня.

И в хорошем таком настроении,
Отдохнув, благодарно вновь в путь
Поднимается солнце – строения
Гнут под ним свои плечи чуть-чуть.

Солнце всех на земле привечает.
А я в детстве не знал, что оно
Чай калмыцкий так пьет и встречает
Красным цветом ойрата давно.

Перевела Римма Ханинова

Хоньна Михаил
ХАЛЬМГ ЦӘ УУДГТАН НАРН...

Өрүн чилгрәр нарн йовхларн
Өнгәһәд терз тусм ирнә,
«Герт ортн» – гихләм нарн,
«Гем уга, хөөннь», – гинә.

Хальмг цәәд басл дурта,
Толь һатцас толярн сорна,
Хойрадмбидн ик каструль баһдна,
Тиигвчн суха мет улаһад однавдн.

Нарн тиниһәд салькар серүцәд,
Нанд ханад, ормасн көндрнә,
Герин ээм давшж ишкәд,
Гердж хәләһәд, цугтала мендлнә.

Нариг иитглән юунас уладгинь
Насн ахр меддго биләв,
Тиигн гихнь, хальмг цә уудгтан
Түүмр болтлан уладг бәәж.
1966

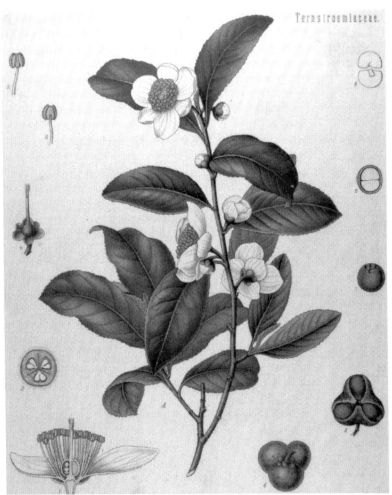

Tea Plant (Camelia Sinensis) Franz Eugen Köhler, *Köhler's Medizinal-Pflanzen*, 1896
Public Domain

THE TEA BUSH
Rimma Khaninova

To my brother, Aita

Some secrets still elude us and lie hidden.
Some come to light again, like the results
of broken vows that reinforce commitment,
quite literally quickening the pulse ...

The Buddhist monk revered as Bodhidharma[19]
dozed off, alas, not finishing his prayer ...
Awakening, he realized his karma:
To keep his eyes from shutting—lest they dare—
he cut his eyelids off and went on sitting.
The rage of weakness helped him in submitting ...

The eyelids, taking root, grew into bushes
that sprouted leaves of magic potency,
and ever since we've drawn on nature's freshness,
partaking of that celebrated tea.

Thus strength is born of weakness on occasion
and to the worthy grants a saving grace—
unquenchably, in all its incarnations,
evincing nature's wisdom without cease.

Translated by Carlton Copeland

---

[19] Bodhidharma was an Indian or Central Asian monk who came to China in the
fifth or sixth century CE and is traditionally regarded as the founder of Ch'an (Zen)
Buddhism.

Римма Ханинова
ЧАЙНЫЙ КУСТ

Брату Айте

Есть тайны неразгаданных секретов.
Есть тайны – всем открыты они вновь –
как следствие нарушенных обетов,
буквально будоражащие кровь…

Заснул монах буддийский Бодхидхарма,
молитве вняв, увы, не до конца…
Определил себе, проснувшись, карму:
отсек он веки, чтобы никогда
глаза не смели больше закрываться –
гнев слабости помог повиноваться…

А веки проросли в земле кустами,
дав вечным листьям силу волшебства,
и в том напитке – знаменитом чае
с тех пор черпают бодрость естества.

Порой от слабости рождается вдруг сила,
достойному прощение даря,
в перерождении своем неутолимо
являя мудрость сущего всегда.
2002

Ханина Римма
ЦӘӘҺИН БУТ

Тәәлгдэд уга учрин нуувч бәәдмн.
Авлдг күчәрн седклд үүмә татдг,
Авшг эвдсн йовдлын ашнь болгсн
Тәәлгдсн чигн учрин нуувч бәәдмн.

Бурхнд мөрглһнд күцц оньган өглго
Буддан гелң Бодхидхарма үргләд унтна...
Нүрс гиж серхләрн, бийән засглна:
Нүднь кезә чигн хаагдшгон төләд
Зовкан хәәрлт уга һар тәәрж хайна—
Зөвтә цухлд бийнь авлгдсн болна.

Зовкнь болхла, бутд хүврж урһна,
Мөңк намчднь илвтә чидл хорһдна.
Зокаста тер ундн – туурсн цә
Мөн, чаңһ-чиирг болхд туслна.

Күчн татуас зәрмдән чидл урһж
Күндтә күүнд геминь тәвж өгнә,
Күцсн әрүн хүвлһәнд эн лавлж,
Күңкл йиртмжин зокал герчлж илдкнә.

Орчулснь Эльдшә Эрднь

67

George is pouring his wife, Rita, a cup of *dzhomba*. Tsagan Sar morning, Howell, New Jersey, 2011
(Photo N. Burlakoff)

DZHOMBA
Rimma Khaninova

Kalmyk tea ... lauded by its people
In proverbs, well-wishes, and in verse ...
Ambrosia's kin, divine in origin,
Though liquid, but excels in taste;
Dzhomba, the mother of Kalmyk food,
The alpha and omega of feast and life.
"Lacking means for drink, but even beggars love dzhomba" the saying goes.
"Let the wood bowl be filled!" exhort
Well-wishers, travelers embarking.
Tea poured to brim, the ancients knew:
Near lip of bowl it needs to reach,
Or guest, offended by seeming slight,
Upends the bowl in sudden impulse:
Censure or rudeness—
Ignominy enough for all.
Let tea-drinking endure for health,
With cup unmarred by evil augur,
Let sun convert the tea, so sanguine crimson
Melds milk and butter into one.
With neither sugar nor honey, a salty tea:
"Without will there is no strength, without salt no taste."
It quenches thirst at sultry noon;
In cold it warms like beam of sun.

Tea in the bowl undulates, like a crone
The ladle adroitly nestles on the edge
Then bounds twixt cups, like nesting doll,
Enthralling and enticing, as in the Promised Land.
And ten times the Kalmyk morphs while drinking tea,
Hot tea-bowl in his hand,
To him, the eons seem unending
As might the steppes were he a horseless nomad amid salt marshes
He thinks himself to be in Bumba
With Jangar.
One of a thousand epic heroes
Bronze-faced from dzhomba and the tanning sun,
Fearless, as a thousand beasts.

… Tea, preserved by forebears, be as strong
As Jangar's legendary lance in battle.
To endure and thrive may people of the steppes,
Drink their fill of Kalmyk tea!

Translated by Nikolai & Gail Burlakoff

Римма Ханинова
ДЖОМБА

Калмыцкий чай…Воспет своим народом
В пословицах, йорялах[20] и стихах…
Сродни аршану[21] он в божественной природе,
Хоть жидок, но первенствует в устах[22].

Джомба[23] как мать среди калмыцкой пищи,
Начало и конец в пиру или в миру.
«Пить нечего, но любит даже нищий
Джомбу»[24], – так говорили в старину.

«Пусть будет аага[25] полна!» – желали
Добра и благоденствия в пути.
Чай наливая вволю, предки знали:
Чуть до краев не должен он дойти,
Иначе гость, обидевшись на скупость,
Вверх дном вдруг опрокинет пиалу:
Проклятие посудой или грубость –
Позора не избегнуть никому.
Пусть чаепитие продлится на здоровье,
А чаша не щербится там во зло,
Пусть солнцем обернется чай, чтоб с кровью
Мешалось молоко и масло заодно.
Без сахара и меда, чай соленый:
«Без воли силы нет, без соли вкуса нет»[26], –

---

[20] Йорял – благопожелание.

[21] Аршан – божественный нектар.

[22] «Хотя чай и жидкий, он первое угощение» – калмыцкая пословица.

[23] Джомба – калмыцкий чай лучшего приготовления.

[24] «Пить нечего, а любит джомбу» – калмыцкая пословица.

[25] Аага – деревянная пиала.

[26] «Без воли силы нет, без соли вкуса нет» – калмыцкая пословица.

Он жажду утолит и в полдень знойный,
Как будто солнечным лучом в мороз согрет.
Чай в пиале кочует, поварешка
Старушкой ловко приютилась на краю[27],
Запрыгивает в чашки, как матрешка,
Зовет зазывно, словно бы в раю.
И десять раз меняется за чаем
Калмык с горячей пиалой в руках[28],
И кажется ему — век нескончаем,
Как степь бесконному в глухих солончаках.

И кажется, он в Бумбе[29] у Джангара[30],
Один из тысячи его богатырей,
Бронзоволицых от джомбы, загара,
Бесстрашных, точно тысяча зверей.

…Чай, сохраненный предками, будь крепким,
Как легендарное его копьё в боях.
Чтоб род степной продлился, был нередким, —
Пей чай калмыцкий вволю в пиалах!
2008

---

[27] «Коренастая старуха подпрыгнула на верх кибитки. (Половник)» —
калмыцкая загадка.

[28] «Пока выпьет чашку чая, десять раз изменится» — калмыцкая поговорка.

[29] Бумба — обетованная страна в калмыцком эпосе «Джангар».

[30] Джангар — эпический хан-герой.

Ханина Римма
ЖОМБА

Хальмг цə...йөрəлд, үлгүрт,
Ханлтта шүлгт эн магтгдла...
Шимтə аршан мет, əмтəхн,
Шиңгн болвчн, хотын дееж.
Хальмгин хот ахлдгнь – жомба.
Энүгəр ямаранчн керг йөрəлhж
Эклнə, күцхлəнь – төгснə.
"Унх уга бəəж – жорасг,
Уух уга бəəж – цəəсг".
Тиигж залхун заң илдкж,
Теегт кезəнə келдг билə.
"Ааhтн дүүрң болтха", – гиж
Амр жирhл мөрəдж йөрəнə.
Ааhд цə кехлəрн, өвкнр
Амн күртлнь дүүргж кедмн.
Эс гиж гиич hундад,
Ааhиг кемрəд чигн оркхмн:
Ааhар эс гиж уурар
Энүнə харалнь hархла – зута.
Аршан жомба цогц батрултха,
Ааhнь харшлж бичə кемтртхə.
Алтн өңгтə шарh нарнд
Айта, зандрсн цə хүвртхə.
Давста, əмтəхн биш, цə:

73

"Күсл уга – күчн уга,
Давсн уга – амтн уга", –
Күчр hаңд унд хәрүлнә,
Киитнлә нарнд ээгдсн болнач.
Түргн эмгн мет, шаңh
Ааhта цәәhин хажуд хорhдна.
Ааhд эн шунж орна,
Таралңд мет үрвр кенә.
Халун жомбаhан ун бәәж,
Хальмг арв дәкж хүврнә.
Мөрн угаhар йовхшң, түүнд
Мөңк болж цаг медгднә.
Бумбин орнд, Җаңhрин өргэд
Баатрмудын негнь болж медгднә.
Чирәнь жомбаhас күрң өңгтә.
Чидлтә эдниг дурасн болна.

...Тууҗд өвкнр хадhлсн цә,
Түүнә жидшң, агта бол.
Алдр тохмчнь батрхин төлэд –
Агч ааhд цәәhэн эдл!

Орчулснь Эльдшә Эрднь

***

Rimma Khaninova

It's often said there's no disputing taste,
And Pushkin's travel notes are confirmation:
Our poet wasn't thrilled, to say the least,
And didn't find an ounce of inspiration
In tea with milk and salt and mutton fat.
A Kalmyk maiden handed him the dipper.
He held his breath – or tried to – after that
Until he saw the mountaintops aglitter.
This unsuccessful picnic breakfast made
His Circe of the steppes no less bewitching.
He found a prose austere and was constrained
To educate his palate just a smidgen.[31]

Translated by Carleton Copeland

---

[31] Pushkin took refreshment in a Kalmyk yurt on his way south to join the Russo-Turkish War in 1829. His distaste for Kalmyk tea and fancy for the young woman who offered it to him are described in his travel notes and *A Journey to Arzrum* as well as in his poem "To a Kalmyk Maiden."

Римма Ханинова
***

На вкус и цвет друзей, известно, нет.
Заметки Пушкина тому вновь подтвержденье:
Не высказал приязни наш поэт —
Калмыцкий чай не вызвал вдохновенья.
С бараньим жиром, с солью, с молоком
Из рук калмычки ковшиком он принял —
И перевел дыханье лишь с трудом,
Вершины гор кавказские завидев.
Сей злополучный завтрак пикника
Нет, не затмил степной Цирцеи обаянья,
Суровой прозе вняв, поэт слегка
Обогатил гастрономическое знанье.
2001

Ханина Римма
***

Кев-янзарн негдсмн гиж
Күүнэ тускар келхд берк.
Амт медхиг, өңг медхиг
Алдр Пушкин бичэд батлҗ.
Хальмг цэ урмдулсн уга,
Ханлтан шүлгч өргсн уга.
Шуурмгар тослсн, давста, үстэ
Шаңhта цээг күүкн бэрүлнэ,
Ууhад оркхла, кинь давхцад,
Уулын ора үзгдсн болна.
Тер өрүни хальмг цэ
Теегин сээхлэг халхлсн уга,
Нүүдлэр бээсн эгл улсын
Негл хотын амтынь медвэ.

Орчулснь Шутран Вера

"The Steppe-Loving Kalmyk," 1983. Polychome.
Garri Rokchinski (1923-1993)

PUSHKIN TEXTS
Rimma Khaninova

The poet wrote "To a Kalmyk Maiden"
When, true to form, habit
Drew him to a pretty nomad's tent,
Bidding goodbye to her, he thought, forever.
Never noticing the family, at breakfast
Round the dwelling's trivet fire,
Noting only a wild beauty,
With pipe, sewing trousers.
Not bad-looking, dark-skinned,
Cheeks—deep blushed—and pearly teeth,
Crimson lips (no thoughts of Petersburg now!)
A kiss—to sweeten the encounter.
But, no—not lips, only her pipe
Circe offers the guest, as a sign of goodwill.
The words resound, in stranger's memory:
("Must not, it's shameful") are burned in.
Her voice is extraordinarily pleasant to the ear,
The poet did not catch her name,
Drank tea, alien to stomach and to soul,
Chased down with mare's flesh jerky as custom deems correct.
Fancied a reward his right,
Proud beauty, though, repaid him
Without qualms--her balalaika
Met his head-ouch!
Wearied of Kalmyk courtesy,
He left the tent, approached the stallions
While they were harnessed, suffused
In reveries of Petersburg ladies.
Her eyes, of course, were dark and narrow,
Her nose was flat and forehead wide,
She never prattled in French or pressed
Her legs in with silky glide.
And never sliced bread by the samovar
In pretty patterns *à l'anglaise,*
And never raved about Cinq-Mars

Or fancy Shakespeare overpraised.
She didn't fall into reverie
Whenever her sweet head was empty,
Or gallopade in the Assembly,
Delight in warbling *"Ma dov'è"*
But why did all this matter? The poet was spot on,
He noted, for precisely one half hour,
In heart and mind the maiden's eyes
Were less than beautiful.
But, still, within a week
He amended his notes,
In which we comprehend in deed
The mockery of Pushkin's tongue.
Pushkin's flirtation with the Kalmyk,
Could be a keepsake album poem,
Forever hence our key to
How the wanderer saw the steppes.
The poet's cry--
To forget oneself, frivolous soul,
With whom, and where, is all the same to us,
To us, is not a whimsy from that time on.
In glittering hall, in modern loge
Or nomad's wand'ring tent--
"plus ça change,"
There Pushkin's profile is alive.
This poetic marathon,
Has burst into our new age,
Crowding out Tyutchev and Fet
Restarting the alphabetic heat.
We bid the poet "adieu,"
Not "good bye," we wish,
For the ephemeral buss
To that great-granny we are thankful.
Oh, nameless one, with trousers,
Your pipe in blossom-lips,
And tea cup, eternally you are with us:
You did not forget honor and modesty.
And joy bursts out again:
For half an hour.
You inspired his Word:
How playful are the Heavens!

Translated by Nikolai & Gail Burlakoff

Римма Ханинова
ПУШКИНСКИЕ ТЕКСТЫ

Поэт писал: «Любезная калмычка»,
Прощался с ней, как думал, на века,
Когда его похвальная привычка
Вслед за кибиткой милою влекла.
Семейства он в кибитке не заметил
За завтраком вкруг там, у тагана, –
Одну красу он дикую приметил,
Портки что шила, с трубкой у огня.
Так недурна собою, смуглолица,
С румянцем темным, зубы – жемчуга,
Багровы губки (что теперь столица!),
Поцеловаться б – встреча дорога.
Но нет, не губки, а свою лишь трубку
Цирцея гостю в знак добра дает:
И в памяти пришельца вновь зарубку
(«Неможна, стыдно») слову задает.
Приятен голос чрезвычайно слуху,
Поэт не понял, как ее зовут,
Пил чай, чужой желудку, да и духу,
И кобылятиной заел: обычай чтут.
Подумал о правах вознагражденья,
Но гордая красавица его
Своею балалайкой без стесненья
По голове приветила – ого!
Калмыцкая любезность надоела,
Он выбрался к коляске и к коням,
Пока их запрягали, то и дело
Припоминал он петербургских дам.
Ее глаза, конечно, темны, узки,
И плосок нос, и лоб ее широк,
И не лепечет вовсе по-французски,
И шелком не сжимает она ног.
По-англицки она пред самоваром
Узором хлеба может не крошить,
Не восхищается она Сен-Маром,

81

Слегка Шекспира может не ценить.
Не погружается в мечтанье,
Когда нет мысли в голове,
Галоп не прыгает в собранье,
Не распевает арий: Ma dov'é.
Что нужды в том? Поэт был точен,
Отметил, ровно полчаса,
В уме и в сердце – девы очи,
Не первобытная краса.
Но все же он через неделю
Перебелил свой черновик,
В котором мы узнаем в деле
Бурлескный пушкинский язык,
Кокетство Пушкина с калмычкой,
Почти альбомный мадригал,
Что стал навеки нам отмычкой,
Как странник степи постигал.
И восклицание поэта –
Забыться праздною душой,
Не все ль одно: и с кем, и где-то –
Не безразлично нам с тех пор.
В блестящей зале, в модной ложе
Или в кибитке кочевой
Везде мы видим снова то же:
Там профиль пушкинский – живой.
И вот посланья эстафета,
Уже ворвалась в новый век,
Тесня и Тютчева, и Фета,
На алфавитный вновь забег.
И мы поэту «до свиданья»,
А не «прощай» всё говорим,
За мимолетное лобзанье
Прабабки той благодарим.
О, безымянная, с портками
И с трубкой в лепестках-устах,
И с ковшиком, ты вечно с нами:
Ты не забыла стыд и страх.
И распирает гордость снова:
Тогда в степи на полчаса
Ты вдохновила его Слово:
О, как шутливы Небеса!..
2008

Ханина Римма
ПУШКИНӘ ТЕКСТС

Гейүрсн бийинь сәәхн авъяснь
Гериннь ардас дахулсн кемлә,
Хаһцад, мөңкинд салҗасар, шүлгч:
«Хальмг һольшг күүкн», – бичлә.
Өрүн герт, тулһин өөр,
Өрк-бүлинь оньһсн уга, –
Заядар һанзта, шалвр уйҗасн
Зерлг сәәхләг эн үзнә.
Уйн, хар шарвцр чирәтә,
Улавр халхта, сувсн шүдтә,
Урлнь улан(хотл балһсн юмбв?)
Үмсхнь бәәж – харһлт ховр.
Болв урлан биш, һанзан
Бишркг күүкн гиичд бәрүлнә.
Хәрин күүнә тодлврт эн
(«Болшго, ичр») үгинь темдглнә.
Дунь чикнә хуҗр хаңһана,
Неринь шүлгч медсн уга.
Терүнә геснднь, сананднь чигн
Төрүц зокшго цә уула.
Мөрнә борцлсн мах идлә.
Бийинь ачлх гиҗ санла:
Болв караг сәәхлә домбрарн
Болһамҗ угаһар толһаһарнь цокна!
Хальмг күүкнәс зулад эн
Тергн, мөрд талан йовла.
Тедниг белдәд татҗасн кемд
Петербургин күүкд улсиг санла.
Терүнә нүднь лавта уутьхн.
Хамрнь хамшһр, маңнань өргн,
Кевшҗ парнцсар эн келхш,
Кеерч, көлән торһар бүтәхш.
Самоварин өмн англин бәрцәр
Салһҗ, нимгнәр өдмг утлхш.

Сен-Мариг легд буульхш,
Шекспириг әрвжго медсәр магтхш.
Толһад үүл уга цагла
Тоолад айстан уха туңһахш.
Наадад «Ma dov'é» дуулхш.
Нәәрин көлд биилж өсрхш.
Ямр төрв? Шүлгч лигтә.
Ямлж темдглв: өрәл частан
Энүнә седклднь – күүкнә нүдн,
Экн цагин сәәхн биш.
Болв долан хонг давхла,
Бичгин харан цеврәр бичв.
Туурсн Пушкинә шогч келнь
Түүнд маднд ил медгднә.
Айтахн күүкнлә Пушкинә эркллһн,
Альбомн мадригалла шаху болм,
Зуучлач күн яһж тeeгиг
Зууран медсинь тәәлдг түлкүр.
Серглң шүлгчин бахтж дуудлһн –
Седкл амр альд, кенлә
Сергж аадрсн эс әдлий –
Тер цагас авн маднд
Төрүц йилһл уга биш.
Өргән ширәдчн, ишкә гертчн,
Альд болвчн дүринь үзнәвидн:
Берк билгтә Пушкин әмд.
Бачм эн илгәцин эстафет
Шин зун җилд орв.
Алдр Тютчевиг, Фетиг шахҗ,
Алфавитн урлданд орхар зүткнә.
Шүлгчд «Менд бәәтн» гихшвидн,
«Шинәс харһий» гиж дурднавидн.
Тeeгт кезәнә элнцг ээжим
Теврәд үмсснднь ханлтан өргнәвидн.
О, эс таньгдсн, һартан шалврта,
Делв-урлдан һанзта, шаңгта,
Чи мөңкинд маднла бәәнәч:
Чичрәд, ичрән геесн угач.
Чееж дәкнәс байрар дүүрнә:
Тeeгт , өрәл част, кезәнә
Таңсг шүлгчд сүрә өгләч:
О, теңгр, ямаран шогтач!..
Орчулснь Эльдшә Эрднь

TEA AND TEA BOWL
Rimma Khaninova

People drank, and will continue to drink, tea,
Black, green, and other kinds,
Ostensibly faithful to ceremonies, but it seems
One's own, the Kalmyk tea, is not in fashion.
Nutmeg, milk, tea leaves,
With, oil, salt, and water from a spring--
All that is yesterday; this cookery
Is meant, perhaps,
For grannies and graybeards.
The young drink «Nestea», «Coca-Cola»,
And «Pepsi», and different chocolates,
While others master teachings
about imported teas.
Japanese tea, Chinese tea with their tea service,
With jasmine, or with lemon, in a kimono,
Only such tea will rate a visa to the table,
Exoticism excites—like movies.
English tea, that is so dignified, with
Oatmeal, jam, toast, and orange,
Teapot, cup with saucer—it is apparent
That the Old World made a visit.
And mugs with graphics, images,
Of unimaginable size and colors,
Like invaders, dug-in in bags,
On shelves, and cupboards of all sorts.
Forgettable, disposable tableware
Flows into trash; why pity it?
Our tea bowls also saw misfortune,
Preserving forebears' stories for many years.
That one, the wooden one, is long since on display;
Faience and porcelain are still in style.
But we are more disdainful, meaner,
To the family's cups on oilcloth-cover'd tabletops;
We part with them without regret,

85

Faded and cracked long ago,
To superstitions we readily respond:
It's time to be rid of them. There is no room, in any case.
There seems to be no place for such wares.
Exception proves the rule,
We moderns need no such cares,
Or repentances at holiday dinner table.
Father is gone, his cup departed;
In dictionary only is the proverb still alive.[32]
Unquestioning, mundane fatigue ...
Which century wafts outside?

Translated by Nikolai Burlakoff

---

[32] The reference here is to the Kalmyk saying: "When the father dies, his cup remains as a memorial."

Римма Ханинова
ЧАЙ И ПИАЛА

Чай пили, пьют и будут пить народы,
И черный, и зеленый, и любой,
И церемонии послушны бы, но вроде
Не моден чай калмыцкий свой, родной.
Орех мускатный, молоко, заварка,
Да масло, соль, вода из родника –
Все это день вчерашний, эта варка,
Быть может, для старушки, старика.
А молодежь пьет «Nestea», «Кока-колу»
И «Pepsi», и различный шоколад,
Иные же осваивают школу
Того же чая, но там импортный расклад.
Чай по-японски, по-китайски с их сервизом,
С жасмином ли, лимоном, в кимоно,
Такой лишь чай к столу получит визу,
Экзотика волнует: как в кино.
Чай по-английски – это так солидно:
Овсянка, джем, и тост, и апельсин,
И чашка с блюдцем, чайник – сразу видно,
Что Старый свет нас тоже посетил.
А кружки с письменами и рисунком
Немыслимых размеров и цветов,
Как оккупанты, окопались в сумке,
На полке и в буфете всех родов.
Посуда одноразова, безлика,
Потоком в мусор, что ее жалеть?
А пиала видала тоже лихо,
Хранила память предков столько лет.
Та, деревянная, давно уже в музее,
Фаянс, фарфор по-прежнему в цене.
Но равнодушнее ли, злее
К семейным чашкам на клеенчатом столе,
Мы расстаемся с ними без печали:

И выцвели, и треснуты давно,
И суевериям охотно отвечали:
Пора их выкинуть, нет места все равно.
Нет места, видимо, нигде такой посуде,
А исключение лишь в правиле одном,
И не нужны нам, современным, пересуды
И покаяние за праздничным столом.
Отца уж нет, и чашки не осталось,
Пословица живет лишь в словаре.
Казалось бы, житейская усталость…
Какое из столетий во дворе?
2008

Ханина Римма
ЦӘ БОЛН ААҺ

Күн дурлҗ цә эдлнә:
Көк, хар ямаран чигн.
Эдниг уудг заңшал тевчнә,
Этүдәр шинҗлхнь, мана баһчуд
Эврә хальмг цәәһән һолна.
Зәт, үсн, цә, тосн,
Давсн, булгин усн – эн тоот
Давҗ мартгдсн хот, ода
Зүгәр медәтнр иигҗ болһна.
Баһчуд болхла, «Pepsi», «Nestea»,
«Кока-кола», олн зүсн шоколад ууна.
Баһчудын зәрмнь цәәд дурлвчн,
Талын орна заңшалд шүлтнә.
Китдин, японя ааһ-савта йосрхл
Кимоно өмссн, лимонта, жасминтә болна.
Тиим цә эдлхд тааста,
Тертн кинод үүмүлдг экзотик мет.
Англь цәәһин тууҗнь тоомсрта:
Апельсин, суль, джем, шарчксн өдмг,
Тәрлктә ааһ, чееньг – энтн
Талын орн-нутгин шинҗ.
Бичмртә, зургудта кружкс болхла,
Биирәр ширдсн эдн – сумкиг,
Кесг зүсн буфетмүдиг, тагтыг,
Күчәр гилтә эзләд авцхаж.
Негхн эдлвртә ааһ-савиг
Нам төрүц харм биш.
Агч ааһ зовлң үзлә,
Алдр өвкнрин тодлвр хадһлна.
Эн ааһ кезәнә музейд,

Эдлврт – мөөлүр, шаазӊ ааhс.
Болв ширә деерк ааhстаhан
Бидн хармнл уга салнавидн:
Кемтркә, өӊгән геесн эдниг
Кезәнә сүзглҗ хайх кергтә.
Тиим ааh-савд эндр
Төрүц зә уга бээдлтә.
Болв маднд хов зөөhәд,
Бийән гемшәhәд керг уга.
Эцкм уга, ааhнчнь уга,
Үлгүр зуг тольд хадhлгдна.
Уйдад муурв гиҗ санхм...
Эндр ямаран зун җилв?

Орчулснь Эльдшә Эрднь

90

EXPLANATORY MATERIALS

"Dzhungariya," 1990. Polychrome. Garri Rokchinski (1923-1993)

HISTORY AND VIEWS OF KALMYK TEA
Nikolai Burlakoff

The argument advanced in this work is that Kalmyk tea plays an important role in the cultural life of that people. Historically, however, it was also an important food item in everyday life. The ease of storage, simplicity of preparation, caloric content, and its stimulative qualities and ability to warm or cool, depending on the weather, made it an ideal food. The tea initially came to the Western Mongol Oirats[33] (the precursors of modern Kalmyks) from Eastern (Khalka) Mongols and Tibetans. Tibetans and the Khalka Mongols, in turn, acquired the tea from the Chinese, who traded the tea for horses. Trade was a way in which the Chinese tried to contain Tibetan and Mongol aggression during the Tang (618-907), Song (960-1279), and Ming (1368-1644) dynasties. By the 17th century, when the Kalmyks, led by Kho Orluk, the Torghut Khan, entered Russian lands and then settled north of the Caspian along the Volga, Kalmyk tea had been part of life of Western Mongols for centuries. One of the first outsiders to describe the making and consumption of Kalmyk tea was the Polish nobleman, traveler, writer, ethnographer, and honorary member of the Russian Imperial Academy of Sciences, Jan Nepomucen Potocki (1761-1815). He wrote about encountering Kalmyk tea in his travels in 1797: "Kalmyks cook this tea with milk and butter, making it, in this manner, a healthy and invigorating drink. All the Tartars accepted this tradition."[34]

The evolution of *dzhomba* from its primacy as a food with important ritual aspects to that of a symbolic item whose nutritional aspect is secondary is most clearly perceived through the growth of its role in

---

[33] The relationship of Oirat to Kalmyk is similar to that of Italian to Roman.
[34] Jan Potocki. *Voyage dans les steps d'Astrakhan et du Caucas*. Paris: Merlin, Libraire. 1829. I, 64-65.

secular literary culture, as the culture changed from pastoral nomadism to an urban and secularized one. That change was slow and largely organic throughout the 19th century, accelerated at the start of the 20th, and reached a painful level of change during the Soviet period, particularly during the internal exile of 1943-1957. In post-Soviet Kalmykia the increasing pace of urbanization and globalization created conflicting pressures towards integration with the dominant Russian culture, a felt need for more conscious ethnic identity, and the growth of interest in archaisms such as shamanism. Those pressures created a situation in which Rimma Khaninova's poem, "Tea and Tea Bowl," poses the question of the future of traditional Kalmyk tea and its traditional tea bowl, while at a market in Elista one can buy "instant" Kalmyk tea—"just add hot water and stir." The shift from sacralized food to symbol of community, many Kalmyks believe, can be marked by Alexander Pushkin's poetry, particularly his "Kalmychke" ("To a Kalmyk Maiden") poem in 1829.[35] Pushkin as a central figure of Russian, i.e. Western, literature and sensibilities introduces the Kalmyks and their tea to an outside world. Much of the subsequent development of Kalmyk literary (particularly poetic) culture is premised on Pushkin's experience. Therein lies the history of Kalmyk tea as a symbolic item, subject to different perceptions and expressed views.

Pushkin's contacts with Kalmyks were few. They appear to have been limited to his journey to the Caucasus in 1829, when he passed through Kalmyk areas of habitation, and occasional encounters in St. Petersburg. His works also do not deal with them extensively. The earliest is the 1829 poem, "To a Kalmyk Maiden," that recounts Pushkin's experience with Kalmyk tea, as well as his diary entries about this incident written shortly afterwards, and the publication in 1836 of *Journey to Arzrum*, in which the tea incident is presented in modified form. 1836 also sees a number of other publications in which Kalmyks are mentioned: the historical novel *The Captain's Daughter*, and Pushkin's most influential, but untitled, poem about the role of a poet in society, most often called "Monument." A note about an incident involving Pushkin and a Kalmyk servant, in which the servant refused to identify Pushkin as a source of an off-color joke, and which elicited the quip, "Asia was protecting Africa," is the known extent of Pushkin's connections to the Kalmyks.

---

[35] First published in *Literaturnaya gazeta*, 1830.

Despite the fact that "To a Kalmyk Maiden" predates the "Monument," it is the latter that is most often cited as evidence of the poet's goodwill towards the Kalmyks. It is not surprising, therefore, that a translation of this poem was made by Mikhail Khoninov in the late 1960s or early '70s. (The translation was published later.)

In the fourth, and key, stanza of his poem Pushkin writes that the poet achieves immortality by celebrating freedom and the attribute of mercy in a harsh times. That sentiment of freedom and call for mercy would obviously appeal to a poet like Khoninov who went through the horrors of WWII, subsequent exile, and then found himself in a minority status in his native land. By choosing to translate a major poem by Russia's premier poet, Khoninov eloquently illustrated his faith that the poet and poetry can call for the best in all of us, regardless of the specifics of our individual cultures or times. Translating the poem into Kalmyk also served to symbolically and graphically create equivalence between Russians and Kalmyks. The translation illustrates the interdependence of two distinct cultures that have shared the same lands for over 400 years.

In some ways, Khoninov's translation is a datum point, marking a new direction in Kalmyk post-war, post-exile literature. This is the full-fledged entrance of Kalmyk cultural expression into Soviet cultural space—maintaining its own ethnic cultural specificity, but becoming a component of a larger literary tradition. If one accepts the notion that the fundamental distinction between traditional Russian and Kalmyk ways were not religious or ethnic, but a distinction bred by a nomad way of life—Kalmyk—and a settled agricultural mode—Russian—then the settlement and particular accelerated urbanization since their return to Kalmykia in 1957 creates a more closely shared cultural environment. In this environment, Kalmyk tea, which from time immemorial was a daily necessity of the nomad Kalmyk's life, has instead accentuated its symbolic role as marker of an ethnicity. Beginning the poetic journey of Kalmyk tea with Pushkin's "Monument" in the three languages of this book—English, Russian and Kalmyk—and ending it with Rimma Khaninova's "Tea and Tea Bowl" recapitulates the evolution of the function of Kalmyk tea in the globalized and evolving Kalmyk culture.

Pushkin provided the first known literary responses to Kalmyk tea by a European, first lightly broached in his 1829 poem, "To a Kalmyk

Maiden," and quite concretely in his travel writing, *Journey to Arzrum*, published in 1836:

> The Kalmyks were located near the station huts. Near their gers [yurts] graze their ugly, shaggy horses, familiar to us through the beautiful pictures by Orlovsky. I visited a Kalmyk dwelling (checkered wattle, covered by white felt). The whole family had gathered for breakfast. In the middle a pot was cooking and the smoke was exiting through an opening at the top of the ger.
>
> A young Kalmyk woman, not bad looking, was sewing as she smoked tobacco. I sat next to her: "What's your name?" "*****," "How old are you?" "Ten and eight," "What are you sewing?" "Pants." "For whom?" "Myself."
>
> She handed me her pipe and began breakfasting. Tea with mutton fat and salt was brewing in the kettle. She offered me her bowl. I did not want to refuse and took a gulp, trying not to breathe. I cannot imagine that any other ethnic cuisine could produce something more disgusting. I asked for something to kill the taste. They gave me a piece of dried horse meat, and I was glad for it. Kalmyk flirting frightened me, and I hurriedly left the ger—and departed from the steppe Circe ...
>
> *Journey to Arzrum*, 1836

Both, poem and *Journey* were based on his travel diary:

> ...In recent days, while they were harnessing my horses I went into the Kalmyk ger ... In the *ger* I found a Kalmyk family; a kettle was cooking in the middle, and the smoke was escaping through the opening on top. A young Kalmyk woman, not bad looking, was sewing while smoking tobacco. Her face was dark skinned, dark reddish. Crimson lips, teeth like pearls—need to note that the Kalmyk breed is beginning to change—ancient facial features are disappearing, bit by bit. I sat near her. ... "Kiss me." "I can't—it's shameful." Her voice was extraordinarily pleasant ... they gave me a piece of dried mare's meat. And I swallowed it with great pleasure. After that feat, I thought that I had a right for a reward. But my proud beauty hit me on the head with a musical device reminiscent of our balalaika. Kalmyk courtesy began to bore me and I left the ger and traveled on.
>
> "Caucasus Diary," May 15, 1829

The following sentence was added to the diary on May 22, after Pushkin wrote "To a Kalmyk Maiden": *Here is a message, which in all probability will never reach her.*

The second European literary giant of the 19th century to inveigh on Kalmyk tea was Alexandre Dumas, *père*, the famous French novelist. His thoughts are expressed in his travel reminiscences:

> One of the sons came up to invite us to accept his father's hospitality. We accepted the invitation. When I entered under the canopy of the yurt the head of the family as a sign of goodwill placed on my shoulders a luxurious black sheepskin. This was a gift to me from Prince Tuymen. We sat down in the yurt and the hosts offered us Kalmyk tea.
>
> Oh! This is something completely different from tea! I have never put near my mouth any more disgusting swill. I thought that I was poisoned. This spurred my curiosity to find out what this nauseating drink was made from. The chief thing—a piece of brick tea from China--is boiled in a kettle and milk, butter, and salt are added to it. ...
>
> The prince drank two or three cups with relish, and regrettably I must add that the enchanting princess, with whom one would want to converse only in verse, voluntarily drank a cupful, or rather a wooden bowlful, without a hint of a facial grimace. ...
>
> *Impressions de Voyage: En Russie*," [Adventures in Czarist Russia, or From Paris to Astrakhan], 1865.

While it may be expected that a St. Petersburg dandy like Pushkin would have a negative reaction to an unusual food, a similar reaction from a food connoisseur and famed cookbook author—Dumas wrote: *Grand Dictionnaire de cuisine (Great Dictionary of Cuisine)*, 1873—would be less expected. Despite their negative response to the flavor of Kalmyk tea, these two representatives of European literature noted some central elements in the preparation and drinking of Kalmyk tea. Pushkin reported the presence of the whole family for tea and the tradition of offering the tea to a guest. Dumas also showed the offering of tea to a guest, and that even in the upper reaches of Kalmyk society the tea was beloved. Pushkin noted the centrality of the cooking fire in the Kalmyk *ger*, but he never noted the centrality of fire in the Kalmyk worldview and life.

A modern writer, Leonid Yuzefovich, in *Samoderzhets pustyni* (*Desert Autocrat*), 1993, depicts a much more vivid image of the role of fire in the nomad's life:

> He who lives among nomads knows: 'That it only takes the skilled hand of a housewife, armed with tongs, two or three movements for a grey wad to appear from beneath the ashes. If she pours on it some green powdered horse manure and blows on the smoking powder a flame will break out; and if one were to add to the fire pit a few pieces of dried manure, then before the astonished gaze of the traveler a bright, even flame will flash that will caress the bottom of the vessel in which tea is brewing.'

By 2010, when Nauka, the imprint of the Russian Academy of Sciences, released the book *Kalmyki* (*The Kalmyks*), the description of Kalmyk tea lost all the drama and color found in Pushkin, Dumas, or even Yuzefovich. Instead we have a short, comprehensive, and detached description of tea-making and historic observations about it:

> A special place in Kalmyk cooking was accorded to a milk tea 'tse,' or 'dzhomba,' which also spread among other ethnicities of the North Caucasus and Volga region. The Kalmyks brought the recipe for this beverage with them in the 17th century from Dzungaria. This was not a Kalmyk invention; it was an integral part of the cooking of all nomadic people of Central Asia, but a tea unknown to the peoples of the North-Western part of the Caspian Basin. The tea is a drink cooked with salt, milk, butter or mutton fat, and sometimes with the addition of flour.
>
> Its foundation is the lowest sort of Chinese brick tea which, with the aid of glue, is pressed into tiles that look like bricks (hence its name). As hard as a brick, the tea was wrapped in a thin layer of paper covered with Chinese characters. Brick tea was brought to Kalmyk districts from the northern provinces of China.
>
> The prevalence of Kalmyk tea among the inhabitants of southern Russia in 1797 was written about by Jan Nepomucen Potocki: "Kalmyks cook this tea with milk and butter, making it, in this manner, a healthy and invigorating drink. All the Tartars accepted this tradition."
>
> In the mid-19th century, Nikolai Severtzov wrote that this "is a drink of Dzungarian and Volga Mongolians and Kalmyks. Its use was borrowed only by the Kirghiz who accompanied the nomadic Kalmyks

or were their neighbors in Dzungaria or Western Siberia, and local Cossacks of the Siberian Host. At the start of the 19th century, the constable Vatsenko wrote in "Description of the Kalmyk and Trukhmen People," underlining: "Mornings it is rare that one of them does not drink Kalmyk brick tea." And at the end of the 19th century the Guardian Vladimir Khlebnikov [father of the poet Velimir Khlebnikov] noted that "the Kalmyks drink tea twice daily and in pretty substantial quantities."

The method of preparing the tea was rather simple: a certain amount of tea was cut from a tea tile and then put in a kettle and cooked for 5-6 minutes. Then milk and salt were added to taste. Tea that was prepared in this manner was subsequently strained through a horse-hair sieve in order to "remove the 'shar,'"(the boiled tea leaves). This 'shar' was not discarded, but was squeezed with the help of a special vise ('shakhvr'), and then added to newly prepared tea, not only in the interests of frugality, but to add a softer flavor. In addition to milk and salt, sometimes a bit of butter was added, and prosperous families would add flavorings—bay leaf, nutmeg, or cloves. The tea is decanted with a 'shankh' (ladle) from the kettle to cups from which it was drunk. Often the tea was transferred to a tea pot ('donbo'); before that is was boiled once again. Any kind of milk would be used—cow, sheep, and the wealthiest could even add camel.

In the 19th century the traditional manner of making tea changed somewhat under the influence of other ethnicities. In the so-called "fried" tea, or 'khursun tse,' a flour roux made with mutton fat was added. This resulted in a very thick and nutritious beverage similar to the milk tea of the ethnicities in South Siberia and Central Asia.

Despite my own Western European background, my introduction to Kalmyk tea went quite differently from those of Pushkin and Dumas. I was introduced to it in November, 2010, when my late friend Shelley Blitstein and I visited the Tashi Lunpho Kalmyk temple in Howell for the celebration of Zul, the traditional Kalmyk New Year. After the service we accompanied the parishioners to the community hall and were almost immediately offered white Styrofoam cups filled with Kalmyk tea. Shelley tasted his carefully, and allowed as how this tasted much better than the tea with yak butter he had in Tibet. I, on the other hand, loved the drink and gladly accepted another cup when it was offered.

Perhaps my paternal Don Cossack ancestral heritage predisposed me to the drink. Who knows? Perhaps my introduction to a version of it occurred some time between the ages of six and eight, while Mother, Grandmother, and I lived in a Displaced Persons' camp in the little village of Kirdorf in post-WWII Germany.

Grandmother was teaching me how to make acorn "coffee." During our work grandmother would tell stories about Russia. She told me about the brick tea, used by nomads and poor people in Russia, which in her stories was made up of floor sweepings in tea factories. She was the brains of our "coffee" operation, while I supplied most of the labor. First I gathered acorns from the oaks surrounding our barracks. Then we took off the little woodsy caps on the thick end of the acorns, and peeled off the shells of the nuts themselves. After the acorns were peeled I grated them on the pinhole bumps of our box grater and then Grandmother spread the resulting mass on a baking sheet and placed it in the sun to dry. After a few days of drying we had a quantity of small, hard brown nuggets that resembled small versions of Grape Nuts. These were stored in a glass jar.

When she was ready to make the "coffee," Grandmother would mix powdered milk, which came from CARE packages, with water and a measure of the ground dried acorns and boil this for a while. The resulting slightly brown brew would be served as "coffee." The mouth-puckering heavy tannic flavor of the beverage was reminiscent of unsweetened strong black tea. Only much later did I make the connection that boiling brick tea with milk was the basics of Kalmyk tea making. Even later I learned that people other than Kalmyks use different grasses and herbs to make their version of "Kalmyk tea" and that the Kalmyks themselves, during times of need when tea was lacking, also resorted to various plants and grasses. It was then that I realized that we, without knowing it, had been making a type of "Kalmyk tea."

My experience with acorn "coffee" parallels the stories of war-time efforts in Kalmykia to find tea substitutes, described in Praskoviya Alekseeva's article, "Rasskazy o kalmytskom chae" ("Kalmyk Tea Tales"):

> During the war grass was used for tea. I don't know the botanical name of the plant; Kalmyks called it *Buzhin avha* or *Akhan guy*. This plant with tiny leaves, violet flowers, and tree-like stems, grew in the lowlands. In the Western District (now Gorodovikovsky) it grew near the village of Baga Buurl. It was a large flat valley to which everyone came

from all surrounding areas to get "tea." The grass was first gathered into sacks, then chopped and placed into vats with pressure applied; this turned the mass of grass brown, making it fit to be used for tea. Of course, this was a tea substitute, not the real drink. Similarly, grass was used during the exile to Siberia.

And, while the ready substitution of certain plants for actual tea indicates that the presence of tea, in itself, is not the most important aspect of the Kalmyk tea tradition, the tea's emotional pull and centrality to the self-identity of someone who grew up with it is amply illustrated by another shared tale from Alekseeva:

> In the summer of 1977 a guest from Riga telephoned. This was Uljumdzhi Ulanov, a resident of Riga who, before December 1943, had lived in our village of Iki Buurl in the Western District. The exile scattered us around Siberia, Central Asia, and the Island of Sakhalin. U. K. Ulanov told about himself: "It is not because I wanted to that I spent my whole life outside of Kalmykia. Before the war the family lived on the horse farms of the Don River. I studied in a Russian school and lived in a dormitory. Afterwards, my brother, Khurmche Ulanov (a graduate of the Moscow Hydrological Institute) and I spent several years in Iran. During the period of exile, we lived in Kazakhstan and I finished college in Baku. After graduation I was sent to work in Riga, where I live to this day, now as a retiree." In Latvia he is an immigrant with Russian citizenship. He came to Elista especially to show his granddaughter the land of the ancestors while he has the right to enter Russia freely until the end of the year. He says, "Who am I in terms of nationality? A Kalmyk—I don't know the language, was brought up Russian, married a Russian. ..." The only thing that has remained of his heritage is the drinking of Kalmyk tea. ... He happily informed us that he found brick tea, which he will be taking with him.

This book's Introduction includes Elsabair Guchinova's wonderful description of Kalmyk tea-making in the United States. I had to smile as I read Guchinova's observation about the most extreme form of the Americanization of Kalmyk tea—a tea bag in an individual cup, with dry non-dairy creamer—such a far cry from communal tea-drinking from a kettle over an open fire. Guchinova's book was written in the 1990s. Since that time the "Americanization" of Kalmyk teas has become internationalized. In 2010, when I began work with the Kalmyk diaspora, one could easily buy instant Kalmyk tea in individual bags with milk already included, offered for sale in Kalmykia and also on the Internet.

In her poem, "Tea and Tea Bowl," Rimma Khaninova directly raises the question of the future of Kalmyk tea and the traditional bowl (*piala*) from which it was drunk. The poet notes the falling popularity of the drink and the cavalier attitude shown to the traditional drinking vessel of Kalmyks. The line that reads "The proverb only lives in books" can be interpreted to mean that traditional verbal culture also is on the way out, together with traditional tea and the tea bowl. A causal relationship can be read into that juxtaposition. Neither the poem nor the poet give us a final answer, however, and instead the poems ends with the question "What century lies outside?"

A possible answer to Khaninova's question may have been given in a cooking show initially presented in 2012 and shared on YouTube in 2014. The show, called "Na shashlyki" (Let's Eat Shish-kabob), hosted by the artist and culinary personality Sergey Tzygal, presented an episode featuring traditional Kalmyk dishes, including preparation of *dzhomba*. The guest for the episode was a well-known Kalmyk television personality, beauty contest winner, and former legislator, Alexandra Burataeva. Alexandra, born in Elista, Kalmykia, after the exile period, is a graduate of the Kalmyk State University, a television show host, first in Kalmykia, then in Moscow, and most recently in Latvia and other Baltic countries. She is a thoroughly modern, successful, and cosmopolitan woman. In addition to her many accomplishments, including a number of national awards, she was the writer/producer of "Operation Ulus," a remarkable program about the Kalmyk internal exile which featured the story of the deportation of her parents, grandmother, and sisters.

"Let's Eat Shish-kabob" begins with the host talking to the audience as he prepares mutton for a traditional Kalmyk dish: *guiirta makhn* (boiled meat). As befits a show dedicated to Shish-kabob, the cooking is done outdoors over an open fire. The host continues to cook, and then Alexandra appears on the set and a conversation ensues. Alexandra watches the preparation, offering suggestions and asking questions. But once the host starts making Kalmyk tea, Alexandra corrects his cooking technique and, unable to contain herself, begins preparing the tea. After simmering the tea for a while, adding milk, then a bit of butter, and finally ladling it, she explains that ladling helps the steam to spread throughout the house and "feed the spirits." In the ongoing conversation the topic of Buddhism comes up and Alexandra states that although she is a Buddhist by birth, Buddhism is not a religion, but a teaching that happens to be quite materialistic. The tea is deemed ready, poured into glass tea bowls (*pialas*) and one bowl is symbolically placed as a *deedzhi* (offering) on the "window sill," an offering for "those who are not present." A minor exchange follows as to who the guest is and who therefore must be served first. Alexandra takes the first sip and then hands the tea bowl with two hands to Sergey. As he proceeds to drink she recites in Kalmyk and then tells Sergey that this is an expression of enjoyment of the tea. She confesses that she has not had Kalmyk tea for some time and informs Sergey that he cannot understand the meaning that drinking Kalmyk tea has for a Kalmyk.

In this brief sequence of *dzhomba* preparation, and the even briefer verbal exchange, a number of interesting details emerge. Most noticeable is the contrast between the beginning of the sequence, in which Alexandra Burataeva explains how in her youth her father would cook a large pot of tea each morning, and her admission that she has not had Kalmyk tea in a long time. This contrast illustrates clearly the demise of Kalmyk tea as daily fare. Burataeva's remark that ladling tea creates a steam that suffuses the house and feeds the spirits is not part of the descriptions of tea-making reported by Guchinova or by Tamara Basangova in her article on tea rituals, although Basangova's article tells of "sprinkling" tea upwards with a ladle to feed the spirits of the departed. Perhaps the idea of steam from ladled tea "feeding those who are not there" is an adaptation of the Ukrainian belief that steam from the cooking of borsch at a funeral meal feeds the spirits of the departed.

Most interesting is the claim that the *deedzhi* intended for "those who are not here" is placed on a window sill rather than on an altar. If that practice is widespread it would mean that a major reinterpretation of the tea ritual has occurred. What is remarkable in this short video segment is that the symbolic significance has been retained and ritual, though possibly reinterpreted, has also been maintained. In short, the answer to the question posed by Rimma could be that *dzhomba* is still at the core of Kalmyk life, but in different guise. That idea is further supported by a law passed in 2011 declaring *dzhomba* a national drink and declaring the third Saturday of May as the "Day of Kalmyk Tea."

Pouring Dzhomba On Tsagan Sar,
Howell, New Jersey, 2011
(Photo Nikolai Burlakoff)

KALMYK TEA: CEREMONY AND RITUAL
Tamara Basangova

In the Kalmyk ritual of worshipping nature objects, freshly made Kalmyk tea was used as an offering. A ritual cup was part of sacrificial rituals of consumption, sprinkling, and offerings. Kalmyk tea became part of the honorific repast of white food,[36] apparently because of the addition of milk to it. In the life of Kalmyks, tea is not simply a daily food but also a holiday dish, and because of that it is filled with many rituals. Taking into account the number of ritual acts which accompany tea drinking one can say that a tea ceremony was common among Kalmyks. A housewife who prepared tea would first have to pour the initial offerings, or *deedzhi* (first fruits in sacrificial cups), and place them on the altar in front of the statues. In accordance to Kalmyk ways a guest had to be presented freshly brewed tea and could not be offered old tea. A good omen was when an unexpected guest arrived just when tea was being prepared by the housewife. A cup could not be filled to the brim—that was a bad omen. The housewife would present a bowl of tea to honored guests with both hands, not touching the brim with her fingers. In response the guest was obliged to pronounce an *ioral*—a poetic blessing—after initially "sprinkling the sky" with tea (i.e., sprinkling it upwards with the little finger and thumb of the right hand). In the past, with the change of an encampment, after setting up the yurt at the new spot, the housewife would immediately cook

---

[36] In Kalmyk color symbolism "white" denotes good, while "black" denotes bad. "White food" means the best food [ed.].

tea in order to call together guests and to receive blessings for the new settlement and dwelling.

Tea preparations were accorded magical qualities. It had to be cooked in the largest possible quantities so that guests could be welcomed into the yurt. One could not step away too far from the cooking tea. The water could not be boiled too long; salt needed to be added, and then the tea would be prepared. Tea drinking, as a kind of blessing, was customary among Kalmyks before a long journey. The belief was that performing travel rituals, one of whose elements was tea drinking, brought good fortune to the traveler. Tea was prepared also after occupational rituals, as, for example, after the manufacture of felt, a collective undertaking; this particular tea was called *ishken tse* ("felt" tea). Before commencing tea drinking this blessing was recited:

> At all times let us
> Drink hot and fragrant Kalmyk tea,
> And pleasantly converse.
> Let the consumed tea be good medicine,
> Let all who drink the tea be generous,
> Let all live in friendship and happiness.

After drinking tea the guests were required to make the following statement: *Uusn tse arshan boltkha!*[37] (Let the consumed tea become our medicine—a healing drink).

The act of communal tea drinking, prepared by the bride on the first morning after the wedding, was a kind of focal point of her entrance into a new family in the role of the mistress of the dwelling, and this ritual was also a demonstration of her housekeeping skills. An example of a traditional *ioral* for tea prepared by the bride on the first day of her married life follows:

> Let tea made by the bride
> Always be strong and aromatic.
> Let sons be born to you,
> And to raise and indulge them,
> Let there be much butter.

---

[37] The Kalmyk term *arshan* means ambrosia, i.e. drink of the gods [ed].

May your table always be filled
With delicious food.
In all four seasons of the year,
May all live in prosperity.

Immediately after giving birth, Kalmyk women would drink tea. This ritual of consuming white food[38] blessed a woman's new role as a mother. It appears that the ritual of drinking Kalmyk tea occurs in liminal (transformative) situations, separating such events from everyday life and highlighting their importance. Tea in these instances is an expression of good wishes for a new stage in life. The Kalmyk tea ceremony developed through the ages and has been preserved to our time, remaining unchanged.

In memorial rituals the earth would be sprinkled with tea. This micro-ritual was called *dusal dusalkhk*—sprinkling with liquid—and was accompanied by an *ioral* (well-wish) for the deceased:

Lord of the Underworld
Let this tasty hot tea which we drank
Become fabulous drink for the deceased.
Let him also be full of it,
Let him reach the Pure Land
And let him not grieve for us.

Kalmyk folklore has retained examples of legends and tales that reflect the revered relationship to this beverage and the time of its appearance among the Kalmyks. One of the popular good wishes is the "Tea Blessing." Holiday celebratory meals begin with the serving of tea to the elders who, in turn, recite the good wish, or blessing. Sprinkling of recently prepared tea occurs daily in the following way: the housewife after making the tea stirs it with the ladle (*shankh*). This action, called *tse samrkh* (to mix the tea), had ritual meaning. The ladle in this ritual fulfills the function of *tsatsura*—a special spoon for the sprinkling of sacrifices. When done, the first portion of the freshly brewed tea is used to spray the sky. The tea droplets, in Kalmyk conceptions, would feed the souls of the departed. Later on, this ritual carried the name *shankhar dailkh* (to invoke luck with a ladle), and used the ladle instead of *tsatsura* for spraying. It appears that in this case we have the transformation of the ritual *kishg dailkh*—invocation of luck.

A mandatory ingredient in Kalmyk tea is salt. I. A. Zhitetskii[39] states that Kalmyk tea is "a food made from brick tea" and describes its

---

[38] Literally refers to milk, cheese, etc. but generally means best of foods.

making thus: "The kettle (*tsekhin khaiisyn*), filled with water, was placed on the trivet under which a fire had been started, and while the water in the kettle was heating, the mistress of the house would shave the needed amount of tea from the brick."

Representatives of other ethnicities regard Kalmyk tea as a soup or broth, it appears, depending on the type and quantity of ingredients used: water, tea, milk, butter, and salt. If, instead of butter, a roux made with flour cooked in mutton fat was added, the tea was called *khuursn tse*; this tea was usually prepared in winter. Rendered mutton fat with added bits of meat—*shuurmg* (cracklings)--was also added to the tea. Another addition was mutton meat, normally from the fat tail of a sheep, which results in a filling drink. The tea was also infused with bay leaf and minced nutmeg to give it a special fragrance. Today's Kalmyks use compressed Kalmyk brick tea, called *khavchg tse*, or *shakhmr tse*, as well as loose tea available now.

Kalmyk tea is mentioned in texts of Kalmyk proverbs and riddles. In a riddle, collected by V.L. Kotvich[40] the components of the tea are listed:

On top—dried and fried,
On the bottom—thick and black,
That which gives color—white,
That which gives flavor—greyish-white,
Giving enjoyment—yellow and fat.
(Solution: dried meat, water, milk, salt, butter)

The brick tea used by Kalmyks is mentioned also in a riddle that states that it is reminiscent of the lattice work of a *ger* (yurt).

Texts of the heroic epic *Jangar*, recorded in Xinjiang Uyghur Autonomous Region of China, include the following formulaic expression describing tea drinking by epic heroes:

Unhindered, they:
Dismounted from stallions in the empty
white steppe,
Built a good stove –*zuukha*,
Made a fire from the saxaul wood,
Placed on it a bronze-brown kettle,

---

[39] I. A. Zhiteskii. Ocherki byta astrakhanskikh kalmykov. Moskva: Tipografiya M.G. Volchaninova, 1893.
http://sambookold.ucoz.ru/load/arkheologija/ehtnografija/zhiteckij_i_a_ocherki
_byta_astrakhanskikh_kalmykov/31-1-0-551 Accessed 12-14-2014.
[40] V.L. Kotvich. Kalmytskie zagadki i poslovitsy. SPb. 1905; 2nd ed Elista: 1972.

Cooked a thick, beautiful tea,
Stirring it from left to right,
Added a piece of butter
Of a size only a crow could carry away,
Slurping, drank the thick tea,
Stretched out like a belt,
Reddened like spirea, and fell asleep.

Another formulaic description of tea drinking is shorter:

Taking cold water from a spring,
Starting the stove fire with *saxaul*,
Placing on it
The bronze-brown kettle,
They began cooking beautiful tea,
While stirring it.
Settling in comfortably,
They began to drink it amicably.

Tea drinking for heroes ended with rest, which was described by the formula: *Su met sunad, sukha met ulahad untv gine* (stretched out like a belt, reddened like a spirea, and fell asleep). The first formulaic description of tea drinking contains the method of preparing Kalmyk tea which contains milk and butter. The weight of the butter is indicated: *kere daam* (that only a crow could carry away).

Tea is one of the Kalmyks' ethnic treasures, their ethnic food, and also a feature of family, occupational and social rituals. This is sacred food which is capable, when rituals are enacted, of transforming the life of a nomad herder and positively influencing life's events.

Tea brick presented to Tsar Nicholas II in 1891
(Public domain, Wikipedia)

TEA IN RUSSIA, PRESSED TEA, AND "MONGOLIAN" BREWING
Nikolai Burlakoff

> It was getting dark; shining on the table,
> Hissed the evening samovar,
> Heating the Chinese teapot;
> Light steam curled beneath it.
> Poured by Olga's hand,
> Among the cups dark jets
> Of fragrant tea were streaming,
> And the boy was serving cream.
> *A.S. Pushkin*

Tea came to Russia in the 17th century. In 1638 Tsar Michael Fedorovich received as a gift from the Mongol Altyn Khan approximately 150 pounds of tea. It's not clear what happened with that gift, but it is doubtful that it was much appreciated, since the Tsar's envoy, Vassili Starkov, tried to talk the Khan out of making the gift. But this event represents the first documented introduction of tea into the Muscovite (Russian) Kingdom. Later, the Chinese ambassador gave tea as a gift to Tsar Alexis Mikhalovich (1645-1676). The use of tea spread very gradually and only among the upper classes, in part because of its extreme expense, in part because initially the Russian Orthodox Church frowned on its use.

After the signing of the treaty of Nerchinsk (1689), the famed Tea Route was established to bring tea to Russia from China. The Tea Route continued to operate until it was largely replaced by the Trans-Siberian Railroad at the end of the 19th century. Four place names are renowned for being centers of the tea trade: Kyakhta, the first center for Russian-Chinese trade; then the Irbit Fair in Siberia; the Makaryev Fair on the Volga; and the famous Nizhniy Novgorod Fair. In 1869, when the Suez Canal opened, Odessa also became an important tea-trading city and the capital of selling counterfeit and adulterated tea. A favorite gambit was to add small bits of metal to add to the overall weight of a lot of tea.

Tea was traded by the so-called *chainiky* (literally, "tea-ers") and it came in special leather-covered barrels, called *tsybiki,* that weighed between 55 and 77 pounds. The tea was carried by camels in long caravans that took some 18 months to transport the tea from Yunan province, China, to Moscow. The Suez route was quicker, and the Trans-Siberian Railroad cut the travel time to about one week.

The shortening of travel time and the virtually unlimited capacity of railroads and ships meant that tea prices dropped, making the beverage affordable for most people. Two additional factors promoted tea drinking: the inclusion of tea in 1877 as a ration in the Russian military, and the creation of tea rooms, that beginning in 1882. Tea rooms were allowed to open at 5A.M., even before taverns, and became the favorite hangouts of city cabbies waiting for fares. To this day, the term for a tip in Russian is *chainye* (money for tea). Thus tea was brought from an exclusively upper-class beverage to a universal drink.

Two main types of tea were imported. One was loose tea—called *baykhovoy*—related to the Chinese term *bai hoa,* or white blossom. The Chinese term is a reference to the barely flowering buds of tea tips which give tea flavor and color. The larger the number of such tips, the higher the quality of the tea. The other import was compressed green brick tea. This tea is traditionally the lowest sort of tea and includes tea bush twigs and coarse leaves. On the other hand, brick tea is reputed to be healthier than loose, it keeps well, and is easier to transport. Traditional tea bricks came in 3- to 4-pound bricks, which could also be used as a currency, since the weight was standard. The vast majority of green brick tea was destined for use by Kalmyks, Kazakhs, Kyrgyz, and other Central Asian ethnicities. The Slavic Russians used mostly loose black tea, and its tea culture was affected by the properties of that tea, while the Kalmyks, other Mongols, and Muslims in Russia, used green brick tea.

The use of tea by ethnic minorities, particularly the Kalmyks, presents a problem in the common narrative of the history of tea in Russia. The Kalmyks successfully petitioned the Tsar to become subjects in 1608. Since Kalmyks were tea drinkers when they arrived in Russia, their inclusion in the Russian kingdom needs to be seen as the introduction of tea use in

Russia. The Kalmyks were also the propagators of tea-drinking among their neighbors, mostly Muslims of Central Asia. In looking at tea culture in Russia we need to be mindful of two distinct routes of dissemination, one stemming from the Kalmyk experience and mostly confined to the Asiatic part of Russia, and the other that reflects the largely Slavic-influenced segments of society.

In the 1960s, William Pokhlebkin, the most popular culinary writer in the Soviet Union wrote *Tea: Its Types, Qualities, and Use.* This smallish book of some 100 pages became an underground "best seller" among the liberal youth of the time. His description of various teas and the traditions surrounding them was the first inter-cultural description of tea that found wide dissemination in the Soviet Union. Chapter four of the book titled, "Dried or Processed Teas," has a sub-section devoted to pressed teas. Following is his description of the "pressed" tea used by Kalmyks and other Central Asians:

Pressed Tea[41]

When tea on plantations is harvested, and also during manufacture, by-products are always created. These are twig cuttings created during periodic pruning of a tea plant; old leaves and stems, which remain in sieves during the sifting of different grades of tea; leaf debris created during curing; bits of tea leaf; and, finally, a significant amount of tea dust that collects in the tea factories.

The sheer abundance and variety of such by-products has, from the earliest times, evoked a natural desire of people to somehow use them in tea-making; since essentially they differed little from tea leaves but were either coarser, or had a less attractive appearance. It was noted that, for example, the bits are capable of producing a pretty aromatic and a stronger brew than even a whole leaf tea, particularly if that bit was from a good tea. The only requirements for utilizations were that tea bits be made more convenient to use, have substantial form, more compacted and weighing more.

[41] Pokhlebkin's book about tea was first published in 1968 and republished numerous times after the fall of the Soviet Union. The version used here is of the 2001 edition that was the last edition revised by the author, shortly before his death in 2000. *Chai: Ego tipy, svoistva, upotrebleniya.* Moscow: Tsentrpoligraf, 2001. Acessed November 24, 2014 http://www.biblio.nhat-nam.ru/poh.pdf

As for rough leaves, they are of poor quality, which means that more of them (and other bits of tea) must be used in steeping A convenient form—pressed tea—was created by compressing coarse tea leaves and bits. This is how people came to the idea to compress crumbs and coarse leaves so as to make them more convenient for use. Pressed tea resulted. There are two basic types of pressed tea: black and green. Besides them, there is a distinct type of semi-pressed tea—a fermented tea.

The nature of the raw ingredients and shape of molding separate all pressed teas into "brick," "tile," and "tablet" forms. Only the brick form is discussed here.

Brick teas—both black and green—possess all the basic qualities of other types of teas since fermented teas are used in the manufacture of black teas, and unfermented teas are used in the manufacture of the green. Because of the particulars of the ingredients and manufacturing techniques used in brick teas, they have differences in their chemical composition which then manifest themselves in their special flavor and aroma.

In brick teas flavor is most pronounced and aroma is less discernible. A sharp, astringent, earthy flavor is characteristic, with a specific and distinct aftertaste reminiscent of tobacco. In green brick teas this is more pronounced than in black ones.

In the 17th century brick teas (black and green) began to spread in Siberia, and at the end of the 19th 90 percent of Chinese brick was exported to Russia. In the 1930s and '40s manufacture of brick teas was mastered in the USSR, and towards the 1950s and '60s the USSR not only fully met the green brick tea needs of its ethnic peoples (Buryats, Kalmyks, Tuvans) but also began to export it to Mongolia, Laos, and Vietnam, countries that at that time did not get their pressed tea from China and which the mountain people of Indochina were accustomed to using.

Because of climate features and tradition, brick tea is consumed mainly in countries with a dry, continental climate (very hot summers and bitter cold winters), .i.e. in Central and North-East Asia. Under these conditions brick tea did not spoil for years and maintained a high quality. For this reason, brick tea, for a long period in the past, served the peoples of Mongolia, Tibet, and Xinjiang as a means of valuing other things and even as a particular type of monetary unit.

Green brick tea is made from coarse (old) tea leaves, pruned matter, and even branches of the tea plant. The overall quantity of tea leaves should be no less than 75 percent; at times, 25 and even 30 percent can be woodsy matter and green stems.

Brick tea is made in only two countries: China and Georgia. Its manufacture consists of two basic processes—the preparation of Lao-cha (i.e. the semi-finished product) and then the molding of Lao-cha into finished green brick tea. In turn, in the manufacture of Lao-cha two distinct ingredients are utilized—the finer, so-called "facing" and the coarser "internal." The bulk of the tea is made of the latter, with the "facing" (some 20 to 24 percent of the total leaf content of Lao-cha) used to cover the external surfaces of the brick. In the past, using traditional Chinese techniques, the production of green brick tea was a protracted affair that sometimes took a month. The process of creating just the Lao-cha itself sometimes took as many as 20 days! With modern techniques, Lao-cha can be created in 10 to 20 hours, and the whole manufacturing process completed in a day.

The quality of green brick tea is determined by the following factors: first, by the percentage of facing materials (the higher the percentage, the better the brick tea) and second, by the quality of the molding (the tighter the compression, the drier the brick, and the smoother the surface, the higher the quality of the brick tea).

Outwardly, green brick tea is a tile or brick of light or dark-olive color (dark olive is considered to be best) with a rather smooth non-flaking surface on which are depicted not only letters and images are but also complete and undamaged leaves, shoots, and twigs. Edges and corners of the brick need to be sturdy enough so that they cannot be broken by hand. The dimensions are 14 x 6 x ¾ inches, with a weight of 5½ pounds or 5 x 6 x 1 inches, with a weight of one pound.

In China there is a special category of green brick tea, the so-called "log tea," which is made from Lao-cha but in the shape of a log (an elongated cylinder) rather than that of a brick, and not pressed as densely. Log tea contains a smaller percentage of facing material. Its outward appearance represents a rather imposing log of some three feet in length, or a bit larger, and it weights from 16 to 32 pounds (but there are more portable versions of log tea).

Brewing of Kalmyk tea is indirectly covered in his chapter entitled, "Ethnic Methods of Tea Beverage Preparation." The title of the sub-section mentioning Kalmyk tea is "Mongolian and Variant Brewing":

The Mongolian way of preparing tea is similar in principle to Kalmyk and partially to the Kirgiz., which is why it is often called Kalmyk tea in the European part of the Commonwealth of Independent States (CIS), and Kirgiz in Central Asia and Western Siberia; and Karyms[42] tea in the Trans-Baikal region and Eastern Siberia, because the Aginsk Buryats (previously known as Karyms) prepare it in this manner.

This is one of the oldest ways of preparing tea, and its relatively wide geographic distribution, from the deserts of the Gobi and Sahara to the Nogay steppes between the Volga and Don rivers attest to that.

In Russia it was known from the end of the 17th century under the name "Bogdo tea." Its basic ingredients are green brick tea, milk, butter, flour, and salt. Depending on the ethnic composition of the population of an area in which the Mongolian tea was current all ingredients except the brick tea may vary. The milk might be from a cow, goat, sheep, mare, or camel; and butter might be totally absent at times or be replaced or augmented with wheat, rendered fat (beef or mutton); the flour can be wheat, barley, or rye and supplemented with rice, millet, or sorghum. Sometimes, in addition to salt, whole black pepper is added in the proportion of one peppercorn to a glass of tea, and the Kalmyks add bay leaf and, less frequently, nutmeg.

For our understanding of the role of Kalmyk tea it is interesting that Pokhlebkin in the 1960s does not feel it necessary to specifically describe the preparation of Kalmyk or Kirghiz teas. One suspects that his assumption was that this method of tea preparation was well known among non-Kalmyk or Kirghiz Russians.

---

[42] Karyms are mixed-race people of Buryat, Evenks, and Russian ancestry.

THE AAGH, PIALA, OR TEA BOWL
Nikolai Burlakoff

The *aagh*, the traditional Kalmyk drinking vessel (cup/bowl), is usually called by its Russian name (borrowed from the Persian), *piala*. The Kazakhs and Kyrgyz call it *kese*, and it is similar to the Japanese *chawan*. The *piala* is normally round, either cylindrical or shaped like a truncated cone, without handles. Cylindrical *pialas* have a ridge, and are of smaller diameter on their lower part. The vessel's shapes were well-suited to nomadic life; they allowed for compact storage and ease of transport. While seen as a type of cup, the *aagh* or *piala* can be used as a bowl, as it is in China for rice.

In the past, wooden vessels were popular because they were sturdier than clay, and the wood would absorb some tea flavor, adding another flavor element to the drink. Traditional woods used in *piala*-making were cedars and linden. Modern-day *pialas* are made of porcelain, glazed terracotta, metals, wood, or plastic. Tea bowls can be decorated or undecorated. Originally they are believed to have been fashioned from simple potter's clay. It is not clear how long they have been used by Mongols, but it is safe to assume that their use came into being with the adoption of tea in the 7th century.

Besides its utilitarian functions, the Kalmyk tea bowl plays a role in a number of cultural areas. Special cups, *deedzhin tsogts*, are used to make altar offerings (*deedzhi*). But even everyday drink-bowls are intimately and intricately involved in Kalmyk tradition. On the symbolic level, their roundness symbolizes the sun and moon, reflecting the pre-Buddhist sacred spheres. That connection or juxtaposition is made in Mikhail Khoninov's poem, "The Sun Drinking Kalmyk Tea," and in the traditional riddle: "Over ice a silver cup" (Moon). In Kalmyk poetry the metaphor of the moon as a cup filled with Kalmyk tea is common, and a direct folkloric reference to the sun and the tea cup is seen in the following: "All of the people warmed themselves by a fire as big as a cup." Family lore is reflected in the proverb, "When the father dies, his cup remains as a memorial."

Of course, it is in actual tea drinking and in customs associated with it that the cup is most prominent. As Tamara Basangova showed in her article, tea drinking is highly ritualized, with virtually every aspect having

117

symbolic meaning and a traditionally mandated form. Among Kalmyks the tea cup needs to be filled to the maximum possible level without spilling any tea. This tradition indicates welcome, and an attitude of generosity. The Kalmyk practice is in direct opposition to the tea-drinking ways of their Muslim neighbors, who pour only a little tea into a guest's cup, fearing that pouring too much would be an indicator of wanting to rid oneself of the guest. In Kalmyk customs, a tea bowl that is turned upside down by a guest is taken as a curse upon the dwelling, or at the very least an indication that the visitor intends never to return. Even references to time are reflected in *piala* lore: "In the time it takes to drink a cup of tea, things will change ten times."

The *piala*'s deep connection to Kalmyk culture and tradition manifested itself even in the creation of this modern-day book. When I first shared the cover design with Rimma Khanninova, she expressed regret that there was not a tea bowl in the background of the picture. My response was that a plastic cup is the present-day reality among the American Kalmyks. I added that while the idea of Photoshopping a *piala* into the image, to indicate the commitment to continuity of tradition, was tempting, it would not reflect actuality. And I reminded her that, as Buddhists, we need to accept the inevitability of the impermanence of all.

KALMYK TEA RECIPES
Nikolai Burlakoff

There are probably as many variant recipes of Kalmyk tea as there are Kalmyk cooks. And there is no question that over time recipes have been standardized and simplified. In large part, this is due to the change from a nomad pastoral life to a settled one. Gone is the *ger* (yurt) as the center of the Kalmyk's universe, gone is the dried dung fire that helped develop many of the characteristics of traditional Kalmyk cooking. Other historical realities have also had their effect. Among them are the dislocation of a number of Kalmyks to foreign lands after the Russian Revolution and WWII, disruptions of food sources during World War II, the forcible deportation and exile of the whole Kalmyk people during the period from 1943 to 1957, the attempt to standardize and industrialize culinary practices during the Soviet period, and, lastly, the impact of globalization.

Even seemingly unrelated historical events have had a profound impact on practices of Kalmyk tea drinking. The independence of the Republic of Georgia and the subsequent wholesale abandonment of Georgian tea plantations resulted in a substantial drop in green brick tea production and export, which meant that this tea, the mainstay of brick tea supplies during most of the Soviet period, began to be replaced by a resurgent Chinese tea industry. Whole generations of Kalmyks were raised on the flavor of Georgian brick tea and to them "real" Kalmyk tea is the flavor of Georgian tea. The total prohibition on importation of Georgian brick tea into Russia in 2006—a ban that was not lifted until June of 2013—obviously had an even further effect, changing tea habits and tastes.

Unfortunately, I have not been able to find a full description and recipe for Kalmyk tea-making that predates the Soviet period, although such information exists. Snippets of and references to these descriptions whet one's appetite to discover how substantial the changes are in Kalmyk tea culture since the end of the nomadic life. References such as the following, from a description of Adygei culinary practices: *In old recipes the brewing of Kalmyk tea demands a very lengthy period of cooking in a kettle, for example, "until half of the water does not boil-off," after which: "leave overnight to steep,"* motivate one to continue research. Unfortunately, research needs to end and available materials should be sufficient to depict reality at a certain stage

119

of development and understanding.

I used the writings and recipes of William Pokhlebkin as the foundation of the recipe part of this book. A number of factors motivated that decision:

- Pokhlebkin gives recipes for the major categories of Kalmyk tea.
- His recipes are written very consistently, so that any variation is easily noticed.
- Despite his iconoclastic status, Pokhlebkin presents Kalmyk tea recipes using the basic principles developed for culinary writing in the premier Soviet cookbook, *The Book of Tasty and Healthy Food* (1939).
- Pokhlebkin's recipes continue to be published in various formats (usually without attribution) within and outside Kalmykia.

There are problems with using his recipes. His recipes and description of Kalmyk tea preparation appear to be contradictory. For example, he writes: "Usually Kalmyks do not grind green brick tea to a powder, but put pieces of it into a kettle of water ..." but his recipes begin: "Grind the tea ...," or he very explicitly makes a distinction between "brick" as pressed green tea, and "tile" as pressed black tea, but then refers to "green tile tea" in the recipes. More importantly, in the section on Kalmyk tea, as well as in his book in general, he ignores the social, ceremonial, and ritual aspects of the tea culture and focuses strictly on the utilitarian aspect of it. In that, he is obviously a member of the "food as fuel" fraternity and not one who goes much beyond that. This makes his descriptions only partially useful.

In addition to Pokhlebkin I have also added recipes from the Russian-language cookbook *Kalmyk Cookery*.[43] I have included a limited number of recipes from other ethnic groups, in part to show the connection between these cultures and in part to show local distinctions that make each tea culture unique. Some differences are seemingly minor, but so distinct and clear that a careful observer can immediately spot cultural affiliations. To take an example from a different sphere: anyone watching films of Stalin, a Georgian, giving speeches will observe that during a long speech he does not fill a glass with water and then drink it, but instead will splash a bit of water into the glass, drink that, and repeat the process a few times before continuing with the talk. This seeming personal habit is in line with the manner of serving tea among the neighbors of the Kalmyks, of which Georgians are one. A recipe for *bortsek,* a Kalmyk fry-bread that has ritual

---

[43] Shovgurova, Anna and Valentina Alexandrovna Vyatkina, *Kalmytskaya kukhnya* (Elista: Kalmytskoe knizhnoe izdatelstvo, 1986)

significance, is also added in this chapter, since no celebration I have observed in the Kalmyk community goes without the serving of this dish alongside tea.

Pokhelebkin on making Kalmyk tea, from his book, *Tea*:

Usually Kalmyks do not grind **green brick tea** to a powder, but put pieces of it into a kettle of **water** (sometimes, already a bit warmed), in a proportion of one handful (about 1½-2 oz.) to a **quart** of **water** and cook it until the water boils and then add twice as much **milk** (about 2 q.) and **salt** to taste.

This mixture is boiled, while constantly being stirred, for 10-15 minutes. After that it is poured through a tea strainer [traditionally made of horse hair] and the boiled tea leaves have all liquid squeezed out of them.

Sometimes very little water is used, no more than 1-1½ glassful, and the tea is cooked with milk. This is explained by the absence or limited availability in the salt marsh steppes of potable water that could be used for tea. It is this circumstance, apparently, that should be considered the basic reason for the emergence of a tradition of cooking tea with milk among a number of steppe peoples.

Bay leaves, nutmeg, cloves, and only sometimes a bit of **butter** are added, besides milk and salt. As a rule, tea is drunk without butter but with wheat crisps made from dough made with butter.

Dzhomba (Pokhlebkin version)

7-10 oz. green brick tea, 3 q. water, 2 q. cream, 2 oz. butter, 2 tsp. salt, 5-6 peppercorns (black), bay leaf or nutmeg

Grind the tea, cover with cold water and cook on medium heat until it boils, then lower heat and cook for 15 to 20 minutes. Remove twigs that float to the surface, add warmed cream and cook for an additional 5-10 minutes. Add butter, salt, black pepper, cover and allow to rest 10-15 minutes. Bay leaf or nutmeg is added to taste.

Dzhomba (*Kalmyk Cookery* version)

For 10 servings:

1½ oz. brick tea, ½ quart milk or cream, 1½ oz. butter, 1½ quart water, salt, nutmeg.

Cover brick tea with cold water, bring it to boil and boil for 5 to 10 minutes, then add milk or cream and boil, again, for 5 minutes. While cooking, the tea is stirred with a ladle for 2-3 minutes, and then strained. Butter, salt and grated nutmeg are added. Serve in *pialas* (tea bowls).

Khursn tse (with roux) (Pokhelebkin version)

4 heaping Tbs. of green tea, 2 q. milk, 1½ q. water, 3½ oz. butter, 3 Tbs. wheat flour, 7-8 peppercorns, 2 bay leaves.

Grind tea, cover with cold water and cook on medium heat until it boils, and continue cooking for 15-20 minutes. Add salt with milk, then cook flour and butter (roux) to a light-yellow color (do not allow it to overcook) and add to tea with the spices. Serve.

Khursn tse (with roux) (*Kalmyk Cookery* version)
For 10 servings.

1½ oz. brick tea, 1 q. milk, 1 oz. mutton fat, ½ oz. flour, 2 oz. butter, salt, nutmeg

Cover brick tea with cold water, bring to boil and boil for 5 minutes. Add milk and boil for another 5 minutes. Separately sauté flour in mutton fat until it reaches a golden color. Temper the flour with some tea and then add to the sieved tea. Add salt, butter, and grated nutmeg. Serve in *pialas* (tea bowls).

Makhta tse (meat) (Pokhlebkin version)

14-18 oz. fresh mutton [lamb] ribs, 7-10 oz. green brick tea, 3 q. water, 2 q. milk, 2 tsp. salt, 5-6 peppercorns, bay leaf or nutme

Cover mutton ribs with cold water, add salt and cook on medium heat until boiling, then lower heat and cook for 40-50 minutes. Remove ribs; add ground tea to the broth and cook for 5-10 minutes more. Remove twigs that have floated up, add milk, and cook for an additional 5-10 minutes. Add black pepper to taste and serve. Serve the ribs separately, garnish with greenery and boiled potatoes.

Bortslan tse (with dried meat [jerky]) (Pokhlebkin version)

5- 7 oz. dried meat [jerky], 7-10 oz. green brick tea, 3 q. water, 2 q. milk, 2tsp. salt (if the jerky is salty, no need to add salt), 3½ oz. butter (or mutton fat), 3 Tbs. wheat flour, 5-6 peppercorns, bay leaf or nutmeg

Heat water on medium heat until it boils; add tea. Turn off heat, cover pot, and allow to steep. Melt butter or rendered mutton fat in a fry pan. Add flour to the melted shortening and mix everything on low heat and turn off heat. Pour the prepared contents into the pan with water, adding to it cut-up bits of dried meat, bring to boil and continue cooking on medium heat another 15-20 minutes. When the meat is ready, pour in milk and bring to boil. Turn off heat, add black pepper, and let it rest, covered, 10 minutes. Bay leaf or nutmeg is added to taste.

Pokhlebkin on making Mongolian tea:

First the Mongols grind brick tea into a powder and cover 1-3 Tablespoons of this powder with a quart of cold water. As soon as the water boils, they add a quarter or half quart cow, sheep, or camel's milk, one Tablespoon of melted yak (*shar tos*), sheep, or camel butter and also 1½ to 3 oz. of *roux* and ¼ to ½ cup of some kind of grains (rice, millet). Bring all that to boil, again, and to doneness, and add salt to taste. If grain is not used, then only very little, or no salt is added.

Tartar Tea (from the website "About Tea")
http://pro-chay.ru/tatarskiy-chay/

The method of preparing Tartar tea shares general traits with ancient Tibetan recipes and with contemporary Kalmyk tea making. Nowadays this is the Tartar national drink.

It is very simple to prepare Tartar tea.

Take equal amounts of water and milk and for each serving of tea a heaping teaspoon of compressed tea, half a teaspoon of butter or *ghee* [clarified butter] and salt to taste.

Heat the water and when it begins to boil add tea and hot milk. The mixture needs to boil for five minutes, or a bit more. Don't forget to stir. Add salt to taste. Sometimes pepper is added.

The tea is served in *pialas*, and the butter is placed in each *piala* separately.

A variety of ethnic baked goods are served with Tartar tea.

Among some Tartars dinner begins with the serving of tea, and only after the tea is drunk is the rest of the dinner served. But among the Kazan [capital and largest city of Tatarstan] Tartars, for example, the tea ends a celebratory meal.

Regardless of customs, the main adornment at a dinner table is a good conversation.

On a personal note; if you don't have regular pressed tea, this recipe can be tried using a *pu-erh* tea [*pu-ehr* is a Chinese fermented black tea, usually compressed; it ages like wine]. Of course, this is a completely different beverage, but it is very interesting. Try it.

Recipe for Kalmyk Tea in the "Adygei manner"

Take a few stalks (3 or 4) of "**horse sorrel**" [*Rumex confertus*, or Asiatic Dock], rinse it in running **water**, pack it tightly on the bottom of a pot, cover it with water, and after bringing it to a boil continue cooking on low heat about an hour, or until the infusion is a saturated dark color. Then, cover the pot and allow to rest for 10-15 minutes. Remove the stalks with a skimmer or slotted spoon, or decant the infusion into another pot in which you will continue the cooking process.

Add **milk** to the infusion (approximately ⅓ of the volume), and bring to a boil. **Salt** to taste, add ground **black pepper**, and **butter** (4 to 7 Tbs. per pot).

Serve the Kalmyk tea with a ladle, stirring it beforehand. Serve together with baked goods (*Khalyuzh* [fried cheese pies] or *Guubat* [sweet puff pastry with cheese].

Notes:

- To make the tea infusion use only whole stalks with stems, which will not only give you flavor, but what is more important, help keep the stems on the bottom of the pot. Otherwise the leaves will rise to the top and the "cap" will be "unsubmersible."

- If the cold water is first salted, then the extractive abilities of the salt will make the infusion process much faster—approximately twice as fast, and this will save half an hour! In line with that, one should understand that it makes no sense to continue boiling after the infusion has darkened (lost its transparency), since doing so will not make it stronger, but that will diminish its beneficial contents. .."

- The degree of saltiness of the tea depends on individual taste, but in general it should be moderately so, comparable to the saltiness of an ordinary soup, such as an *okroshhka* [Russian cold summer soup with pickle].

- Regarding spices: Normally they are limited to common black pepper, although ground red peppers (sweet or hot) can be added. At times whole peppercorns, or pepper pods are added during brewing instead of ground pepper. Some people add ground coriander.
  To brew tea one should not use aluminum pots; the only acceptable ones are enamel, cast iron, with Teflon surface, stainless steel, etc. One should keep in mind, however, that when the tea preparation is at the stage of being boiled with milk, scorching can occur in an enamel pot.

BORTSOKI

During the past five years, every celebration or memorial service that I attended in the Kalmyk diaspora community was sure to have *bortsoki* as an accompaniment to *dzhomba*. And time and time again, virtually any reminiscence about Kalmyk food mentions the smell of frying *bortsoki* as a happy memory of childhood.

Bortsoki are simple fat-fried breads, similar to the Native American frybread, the Latin American *cachanga* or *sopaipilla*, or the Hungarian *lángos*. In each ethnic group the dough is similar, with some specific adaptations to local ingredients and traditions. One distinction of *bortsoki* in modern times is that it is a ritual/celebratory food and not everyday fare. This is a carryover from nomad times, when flour, the key ingredient, was rare and very expensive. Another distinction is the wide variety of symbolic shapes that are given to the dough, with very specific meanings assigned to each.

Bortsoki are especially important for Kalmyk New Year's (*Zul*). Two shapes are particularly important on that holiday: *tselvg* (flapjack-shaped) and *tohsh* (wheel-shaped). Both represent the sun. The poet Sandzhi Kalyeav also compared the *tselvg* to a lake—water sources being of prime importance to nomads. The wheel shape of *tohsh* represents the wheel of *samsara*—everyday life. There are well over a dozen other shapes, including camel, goose, ram, spear point, reins, mutton intestines, horse's large intenstine, etc. Each has a separate meaning and is cooked for different holidays or occasions. "Reins" *bortsoki*, for example, are a good wish for a happy journey, and I observed them served at memorial services.

Kalmyk foodways did not have soups, hence the rich tea, and they did not have sweets in their diet. *Bortsoki*. therefore, are traditionally made without sugar and are not sweetened with honey, as in the case of New Mexico's *sopaipillas*. An American who tastes this dish for the first time often expects a doughnut taste because of the reminiscent fried-oil smell and surface texture of the bread and becomes confused by the bread flavor.

Each housewife has her own recipe for this dish, but there are only two basic/normative recipes. Both recipes are found in the 1986 Russian-language cookbook *Kalmyk Cookery:*

Recipe 1
2½ c. all-purpose flour
1 egg
1½ cups milk
7 Tbs. margarine
7 tsp. sugar
1 tsp. baking soda
2 tsp. salt
Fat (oil) for frying

To prepare the dough: Combine milk with melted margarine, sugar, salt, baking soda, and egg. Mix. Add flour. Mix very thoroughly. Let it rise for 1 to 1½ hours. Roll out dough, and cut out shapes if you wish. Fry in large amount of very hot fat or oil.

Recipe 2
3 c. flour
1 egg
1 c. milk
3½ Tbs. margarine
1¼ oz. yeast
5 tsp. sugar
1 tsp. salt
Fat for frying

Heat milk to lukewarm (about 100 ° F). Add melted margarine, egg, sugar, salt and yeast. Mix. Add flour to the liquid ingredients and mix thoroughly. Place in warm draft-free place for 3-4 hours to rise. When it doubles in bulk, punch the dough down. Let it rise again. Punch it down once or twice more, then let it rise for a final time. Once the dough is ready, roll it out and cut it into desired shapes. Let it proof (rise) once again. Cook in very hot oil.

As one author wrote in her article about *bortsoki*: "Let us gather once again, enjoying the warmth of our family and the tasty breakfast of a mouth-melting *tselvg* and *tohsh* followed by the aromatic taste of *dzhomba.*"

ON TRANSLATIONS: NOTES AND COMMENTARY
Nikolai Burlakoff

"Three grades of evil can be discerned in the queer world of verbal transmigration."[44] Thus begins Vladimir Nabokov's elegant screed about literary translators other than himself. His acidic take on the pitfalls of bad translations warns of the greatest seduction that a translator needs to avoid: "Instead of dressing up like the real author, he dresses up the author as himself." Nabokov also propounds his "simple" rules for achieving the ideal translation:

> First of all he must have as much talent, or at least the same kind of talent, as the author he chooses. In this, though only in this, respect Baudelaire and Poe or Joukovsky and Schiller made ideal playmates. Second, he must know thoroughly the two nations and the two languages involved and be perfectly acquainted with all details relating to his author's manner and methods; also, with the social background of words, their fashions, history and period associations. This leads to the third point: while having genius and knowledge he must possess the gift of mimicry and be able to act, as it were, the real author's part by impersonating his tricks of demeanor and speech, his ways and his mind, with the utmost degree of verisimilitude.

This is obviously a tough standard to meet, particularly when a book has nine translators, from at least four different cultures, and involves three languages. That being said, translation—both linguistic and cultural—is at the heart of this book. While its targeted primary reader is an English speaker, readers of either of the other languages can enjoy the collection of texts. The book might be most useful to children of Kalmyk immigrants who may not know Kalmyk or Russian, and who may not be aware of the

---

[44] Vladimir Nabokov. "The Art of Translation," *New Republic*, August 4, 1941
http://www.newrepublic.com/article/113310/vladimir-nabokov-art-translation

deep connections of Kalmyk tea to Kalmyk culture or to Russian literary culture. It might be useful also to Kalmyks learning English. Since translation is so important to the work, a few remarks about literary translation are in order from toilers in the field less stellar than Nabokov. Comments that clarify or enhance understanding of some of the poems are appended.

Walter May, a noted British poet and translator-extraordinaire of poetry, wrote in 1965 about the difficulty of translating poetry, and of finding readers for such work[45]. The latter phenomenon he blamed on the tendency of much of the then contemporary poetry to be suffused with emotive and obscure symbols so individualized as to be of interest to few people other than the poet. He failed to note, however, that obscure symbols and extreme individualization are not a problem with folk poetry, which exists only as a result of shared values, poetic images, tropes, and themes. The dearth of readers of folk poetry therefore has other causes.

May attributed the fear of translating poetry to a process of defeatist hypnotization in which the dictum "poetry is untranslatable" had become a self-fulfilling prophecy, abetted by critics. As a counter, he offered Vera Inber's passionate defense of poetry translation at a translators' symposium in Rome in 1963. Inber's injunction was that poets who translate should give primacy to the sense and thought of a poem and not limit themselves to its emotions. This position is reinforced by Yulia V. Sokolova, the senior lecturer of English at the Byelorussian State University, who indicates that poetry translation is the most difficult of a translator's tasks because such an effort must: 1) Transmit the poet's thought; 2) Re-create the imagery and expressiveness of the original text, while retaining its ethnic flavor; 3) Make the accessibility of the translated text relevant to the carrier of a different culture.[46]

---

[45] Walter C. May. "The True Translation of Poetry," *The Anglo-Soviet Journal,* June 1965, pp. 51-56 http://www.unz.org/Pub/AngloSovietJ-1965q2-00051

[46] Sokolova, Yulia V. " Leksiko-Grammaticheskie transformatsii pri belorusskogo-angliskom perevode. Perevod imen suschestvitelnykh" [The Lexico-Grammatical Transformations in Byelorussian-English Translation of Poetry: The Translation of Nouns]. Vesnik BDU [The Herald of the Byelorussian State University] series4, 2012, No. 3. Accessed July, 2014.
http://elib.bsu.by/bitstream/123456789/58107/1/33-36.pdf Ю. В. СОКОЛОВА

There is also, however, a school that believes that maintenance of meter and rhyme of the original are really the quintessence of good translation. That school of thought runs into serious problems when encountering languages where the rules of poetry are significantly different from the original language. For example, in Kalmyk, end rhymes are not distinctive markers of a poetic line, while rhyming of initial words in a line are. In the translations found in this book we have a range of attitudes by the different translators towards formal aspects of poetry. Difficulties arise when the esthetic of the translator and poet differ.

Another set of problems arise when translating poems that have themselves been translated into a language other than the original. For example, Mikhail Khoninov's *KHAL'MG TSE UUDGTAN NARN* was originally written in Kalmyk, following Kalmyk rules of poetry. This book holds two translations of that poem into Russian: one, by Nikolai Kutov in 1977, and the other, in 2010, by Mr. Khoninov's daughter, Rimma, a noted poet herself. Both of the Russian translations were, in turn, translated into English. Although the Russian translations of the poem are similar, each was sufficiently different from the other that an initial assumption was made that they were from different times in the poet's life. Each Russian poem had a different title, which compounded the confusion. Only when he asked about the whereabouts of the "second" original text, did the translator learn that he was already in possession of the one original. For me, there is no better proof than this that a translation needs to be viewed as an original work which, at its best, can be only partially related to the original. It would be fascinating to "know" how far the four translations are from the original Kalmyk—and what was successfully captured.

A significant element that will affect a translation is time. Language changes over time, literary conventions change, concepts disappear to be replaced with new ones. Only a small number of modern Americans know the complex world of sailing vessels or horse transportation, yet for poets of the 19th century references to these were common, shared by nearly everyone in the society. How far we travelled on that path was illustrated in my own experience when I first saw a picture of the Kalmyk guardian-deity Okon Tengri. She is always pictured astride an animal, which I assumed to be a horse, only to learn later that it is a mule. Had I been more attuned to the culture of the 19th century, or Kalmyk culture, I would have immediately recognized the picture of a mule. Fortunately for our collection, the two oldest poems that hearken back to the first half of the 19th century have been translated by translators acutely aware of these issues, and who offered solutions in line with the cultural expectations and norms of the time of those particular translations. Translators are normally acutely aware of "false friends," i.e. words that are close in meaning but have significanlty different interpretations in different cultures.

Yet more complexities ensue when a contemporary poet decides to write a poem that extensively quotes a poem of another time, particularly when the contemporary poet uses diction and devices of the earlier poet's era. The challenge for a translator then lies not only in reflecting the "channeling" of the original author, but also the contemporary poet's contribution. The issue of writing a "replica" literary work was best approached in form of a literary criticism by Jorge Luis Borges in his 1939 "Pierre Menard, Author of the Quixote."

In this pseudo-review of the fictional author, Pierre Menard, Borges argues that Menard's *Don Quixote* fragments, which are word-for-word identical to Cervantes' book, are in fact superior to the original because the "new" Quixote was created in a time and place so different from Cervantes' time. No matter how one views Borges' idea, however, it is hard not to be impressed by Rimma Khaninova's "channeling" of Pushkin's *TO A KALMYK MAIDEN* (1829) and her own *PUSHKIN'S TEXTS* (2008), in which she engages in a poetic dialogue (using Pushkin's words, poetic devices, and lexicon) with the poet, his poem, his travel journal, and the mores of his time. Both Borges, in his essay, and Khaninova, in her poem, struggle with the question of meaning, and Khaninova additionally introduces the question of the immediacy and richness of history as one engages today in the seemingly simple ritual of drinking Kalmyk tea.

The translator of Khaninova's poem, *PUSHKIN'S TEXTS*, did not even attempt to maintain faithfulness to the formal aspects of her or Pushkin's poems. He used Carlton Copeland's excellent translation of Pushkin whenever possible, to mimic Pushkin's voice, and then attempted to follow Sokolova's injunction to "transmit the poet's thoughts" in conveying Rimma's thoughts. The second priority was to transmit the imagery and "flavor" of the poem as close to the author's as possible, while maintaining easy comprehensibility for today's American reader of English.

The task was more challenging because it involved language and concepts of a meld of two differing foreign cultures. This is the area in which the dialogue between the poet and translator was most intense, when their views differed.

Nabokov ends his extensive article on translation by offering to illustrate how his rules, applied to a poem by Pushkin, provide the "ideal" translation. Then he fails to cite a text. The point being (something that not all understood when the article was published): there ain't no such thing as an ideal translation—just as there is no ideal edit, or ideal expression of an inspiration in an author's writing. Honest translators know that, accept their lot, and love their "children" no less than handsome parents love their less than handsome child.

English-speaking readers who have at least some knowledge of Russian literature should be able to enjoy the poems in this book. To fully engage with all the poems, knowledge of Kalmyk and Russian culture and one or both languages is important. To assist readers who may not be familiar with Russian and Kalmyk materials, the balance of this chapter provides explanatory and contextual materials that can enrich and deepen the appreciation of some of the poems.

EXEGI MONUMENTUM

Alexander Pushkin's (1799-1837) untitled poem with the epigram *Exegi Monumentum* (1836) is a key work in Russian literature, since the author, considered to be Russia's greatest poet and the prime example of its Romantic literary tradition, raises the question of the poet's role in society. This poem is in dialogue with the earlier poem, "Monument" (1796), written by Russia's greatest poet before Pushkin, Gavriil Derzhavin (1743-1816). Derzhavin's poem is a restatement (as is Pushkin's) of Horace's Ode 3.30. Pushkin's poem is in a form not otherwise found in his poetry. The stanzas consist of three lines in iambic hexameter with a caesura after the 6th syllable, followed by one of iambic tetrameter, with alternating masculine and feminine rhymes. The theme, distinct formal characteristics, and Pushkin's multilayered ambiguity, found in his best poems, have made this poem the focus of virtually every poet in Russia who followed him.

In our collection, the translation of this poem by Mikhail Khoninov into Kalmyk is important because it was written shortly after the Kalmyks were formally rehabilitated and allowed to return to their ancestral lands after 14 years (1943-1957) in internal exile. The rehabilitation meant the end of the prohibition of the Kalmyk language. Khoninov's translation can be interpreted as an indirect criticism of the government, by showing the long connection of the Kalmyks with Russia, the recognition of them by its greatest poet, and as a proud statement of the equivalence of the Russian and Kalmyk cultures.

Virtually every word in Pushkin's poem can have, and has had, extensive commentary. Here the commentary is limited to only information that will help clarify potentially obscure references.

The phrase that is translated as "Alexander's Column" is ambiguous as written by Pushkin, but it is usually deemed to refer to the column built in 1834 to honor Tsar Alexander, which is taller than the column built by Napoleon in his own honor.

I would not have translated Pushkin's phrase as "Proud Slave's posterity." Literally translated, the phrase reads: "…the proud grandson of the Slavs …" While a dispute reigns as to the origin of the term "Slav," one school has maintained that it came from the Byzantine *sklábos* (slave) and that is probably the translator's meaning. In his poems Pushkin uses the terms "proud" or "arrogant" as adjectives with the term "Slav" in reference to Poles, part of whose territories were in the Russian Empire. In essence, the two lines of the stanza that list the various ethnic groups are a description of the breadth of the Russian land, which stretches from the west in Poland, the north in Finland, the east among the Tungus of Siberia, and reaches south to the Kalmyks.

"Nor casting pearls to swine" is a reference to the Bible, cf. Matthew 7:6, "Give not that which is holy unto the dogs, neither cast ye your pearls before swine, lest they trample them under their feet, and turn again and rend you." It bookends the opening line's references to Mark 14:58, "We heard him say, I will destroy this temple that is made with hands, and within three days I will build another made without hands."

In general, the idea that poets are messengers from Heaven finds frequent expression in Pushkin's poetry, perhaps most dramatically in his "Song of the Wise Oleg" (1825):

"Seers do not fear mighty sovereigns,
And princely gifts they do not need;
Truthful and free is their wise tongue
And with Heaven's will it is in friendship"

TO A KALMYK MAIDEN

In May of 1829 Alexander Pushkin made a journey to the Caucasus Mountains and Erzurum, in today's Turkey, which in 1829 was under Russian control. On the way he passed through the Kalmyk steppes and stopped at what appears to have been a Kalmyk post station, to get fresh horses and have breakfast. The ensuing incident with Kalmyk tea and his young hostess that is the subject of this poem was memorialized as the first entry in his travel diary, started a few days after the events. It appears that at approximately the same time he penned the draft version of the poem. Subsequently, both poem and journal entry were revised. While the poem is not considered one of Pushkin's major verses, some scholars see it as an important experiment in poetic forms and genres. Among Kalmyks the poem has resonated deeply, as we will see.

TO A KALMYK MAIDEN is an epistolary poem addressed to the young Kalmyk woman. It is close in tone and structure to French album madrigals (short, light verse, often dealing with love) that would be part of visiting and party rituals among members of St. Petersburg's society. The incongruity of addressing an epistolary poem to a nomad woman, who would not have an album, and in any case was probably illiterate, is reinforced by listing the qualities that the woman lacks, in comparison to society ladies of the time. There is further incongruity on the semantic level when, for example, "wild beauty" is juxtaposed with "sewing trousers," among others. In short, this poem approaches the literary burlesque—a work that intends to caricature the manners of a serious work—in this case, most probably, Derzhavin's *"Felitsa"* (1782), the poem, dedicated to Catherine the Great, which made Derzhavin's reputation. Derzhavin does not describe the physical attributes of Catherine, but he lists a series of qualities and behaviors that are mirrored in Pushkin's description of the Kalmyk woman.

Derzhavin's poem begins with the lines: "Godlike Tsarevna of the Kirgiz-Kaisatsky Horde!" and is a paean to the Empress, while satirizing her courtiers. The contrast of these lines to Pushkin's "wild beauty" who is sewing trousers is inevitable, and strengthens the idea of a burlesque. Derzhhavin's poem is, in itself, a burlesque combination of lofty and elegant stylistic elements with common images, so Pushkin's poem becomes a double parody. Most striking are the contrasts between the majestic goodness of Catherine and the simple virtues of the Kalmyk woman, most likely the result of her simple surroundings untouched by the degeneracy of urban society.

KALMYK TEA (Bosya B. Sangadzhieva)

Bosya Sangadzhieva (1921-2001) is the first officially recognized Kalmyk woman poet. She was the daughter of Badmin Menkenas, a noted epic singer (*dzhangarchi*). War and the deportation of Kalmyks (Bosya wound up in Siberia) interrupted the development of her writing life. Shortly after returning to Elista in 1957 she began to publish. Her themes included the role of women; love of the native land, particularly the steppes; goodwill; and of course, elements of Kalmyk women's, life such as the *bortsoki* (ritual fried dough) and Kalmyk tea. Her poem about Kalmyk tea became a popular hit song, and she published a collection of poetry under the title *Kalmyk Tea* in 1978.

In examining *KALMYK TEA* some confusion may arise because at least two different versions are available. One ends with the fifth stanza and the line: "A better drink than this I'll never find!" I found this version published on the Internet, among resources for school children: http://librarymou4.narod.ru/chai.htm.

The other version, which is three stanza longer and ends with the line: "Remember Pushkin's 'Kalmyk of the plain'?...," was translated during Bosya's lifetime and therefore should be viewed as definitive, or primary. This version is of particular interest here, because of the reference to Pushkin and his well-known negative response to Kalmyk tea. Why would Bosya, who painted a highly positive picture of the tea, specifically, as it is tasted by a visiting stranger, include a reference to someone who has the reputation of having disliked the tea?

The answer may lie in a memoir piece, *A Place on Stage* (2001), published by Daniil Dolinskij (1925-2009), a poet and well-known translator of Kalmyk poetry:

> She [Bosya Sangadzhieva] accompanied me to my hotel. Having entered an alley, not far from the city's center, I suddenly saw among the trees a small statue of Pushkin. How many times had I driven or walked by, and saw it only now. So I exclaimed: "But, of course, 'the steppe's friend' could not help but thank the Russian genius in this way ..."

Slowly, Bosya turned her moon-like face towards me: "Did you forget his verse "To a Kalmuck Maiden?" You remember: "Farewell, enchanting Kalmyk maid! Though it was never my intent, ..."

"You know," Bosya said, "Pushkin's verses about the Kalmyk woman were not happenstance. He could have written about a Kalmyk woman without being in the steppes—he could have met one in Astrakhan [Russian city near the Caspian Sea, and traditional settlement of Kalmyks involved in caviar fisheries]. He could have met one at the governor's ball; after all, there he met a Kalmyk *taisha* [high Kalmyk nobility] ..."

And she recounted how he arrived in the *khoton*—a settlement of a few dozen nomad tents, covered with white or black felt made from camel's wool. In the white ones, obviously [white is a color of luck, status and goodwill in the Mongolian color scheme.], lived families of the *nojns*, the local rulers, the masters of the settlement, and in the black ones, of course, less prosperous Kalmyks, and completely impoverished ones. Which tent Pushkin and the *taisha* entered is not known, probably, into a poor one. Not too distant from the tent wall, some kind of mix was bubbling in the kettle, the steam escaping through the small, round opening at the top of the tent, through which diffused light fell on the face of the young Kalmyk woman. ...

Bosya continued:

"This? This is tea," the beauty announced. She arose and returned with a bowl and a ladle, dipped the latter into the golden mix, quickly lifted it and poured the liquid back into the kettle. Having done this a few times, she poured tea into the bowl, not quite reaching the edge (this is so that, as the tea is drunk and as the volume decreases, the tea does not cool too quickly).

While bringing the bowl to his mouth, Pushkin sensed that there was an unfamiliar smell. (Perhaps, this was from old mutton fat which is normally used to infuse the tea with, I thought, being a bit familiar with Kalmyk cuisine.) But, Pushkin was Pushkin, and he would even drink poison from a goblet, if it were served by a dainty lady's hand. And—he drank it... And, of course, after this he wrote his epistle to the "Kalmyk Maiden."

"Perhaps," Bosya replied: "But the Kalmyk woman could only read about herself many, many years later, at a time when literacy appeared in Kalmykia and the poems of Pushkin were translated into the native tongue of the steppe dwellers. By that time she read and wrote well in Russian, and at one time even took up the quill herself..."

Bosya was obviously hinting about herself. And, to be truthful, Bosya Badmaeva Sangadzhieva became the first Kalmyk woman to write poetry and prose, and she was given the title of "People's Poet."

At the hotel, as we were taking leave, Bosya smiled and added: "You are not going to believe me, but that 'enchanting Kalmyk maid' was my great-great grandmother."

The key sentence in the quoted passages is: *Pushkin's verses about the Kalmyk woman were not happenstance.* This enigmatic statement raises a question: "Was there something that Pushkin did not share with his readers?" We know, from Pushkin's own writings, that he was an unreliable narrator. The questions that follow are: "How unreliable?" and "In what specific area?" We probably will never know what Bosya meant by her statement, but her own poem about Kalmyk tea, set within the context of this bit of memoir by a friend, can lead to thoughts that perhaps Pushkin was doing more in his verse that writing a parody of Derzhavin's poem or expressing his views about Kalmyk tea. Of course, the possibility exists that the tradition of literary burlesque is just being carried on by Bosya.

WHY THE SUN IS RED and THE SUN, DRINKING KALMYK TEA (Mikhail Khoninov)

Khoninov was born in 1919, his first book of poetry, *Songs of Joy*, was published in 1960, and he continued to write and translate poetry, write prose, drama, and satirical sketches for years. In all, he authored 50 books, many of which were translated into a number of languages. His translations of such major Russian poets as A.S. Pushkin, Vladimir Mayakovsky, and a host of others earned him the "Friendship of Peoples" medal. Two translated poems in this volume, which are based on a single Kalmyk text, *KHALMG TSE UUDGTAN NARN*, present an interesting problem. Viewing them as two distinct poems, guided in part by the difference in the Russian titles and dates associated with these translations, as well as by linguistic characteristics, the editor provided two different analyses.

WHY THE SUN IS RED was interpreted as a modern-day etiological legend in dialogue with A.A. Fet and his poem "I come to you with greeting, ..." (1842) and Vladimir Mayakovsky's "An Extraordinary Adventure Which Befell Vladimir Mayakovsky at a Summer Cottage"

(1920). An emphasis was placed on contrasting Mayakovsky's attitudes to the sun and life with Khoninov's. A close reading of Mayakovsky's poem established a connection of his poem, and by extension Khoninov's, to Pushkin's *EXEGI MONUMENTUM*. The major difference between Mayakovsky's and Khoninov's poems is that the former saw the then contemporary world as the end of the age of Pushkin, while the latter talked of the eternal connection between nature, man, and cultural expression in the form of Kalmyk tea.

THE SUN DRINKING KALMYK TEA was examined in light of the poetic dialogue that occurred between Khoninov and David Kugultinov. Taking a cue from Rimma Khaninova's analysis of the theme of Destiny, as expressed in Mikhail Khonininov's poem, "Three Answers," in which the response to Destiny's question as to what the poet needs was " To drink Kalmyk tea, ..." an analysis was developed connecting Kalmyk tea to the sky, i.e. the sun, and to destiny or fate. In reading this translation, no connection to Fet or Mayakovsky was sensed; instead, a philosophy of life that saw nature and Kalmyk tea (in everyday and sacred uses) intertwined, was postulated.

After completing the translations, copies of the English-language poems were sent to Rimma for her review and comments. At this point it became apparent that both Russian texts were based on the same Kalmyk poem. Rimma responded with a literal word-for-word translation of the poem and some of her interesting observations:

> ... Khoninov's poem is not childish, as in Kutov's translation. Kalmyks would never address the sun with a diminutive—only as a sacred object. Tea also has a sacred meaning among Kalmyks, in color, temperature, and use; it is reminiscent of the sun and its warmth, i.e. life. Kalmyk poets compare the sun and person to tamarisk, *Filipendula*, and sandalwood, in the tradition of *Jangar* [Kalmyk epic]—in which the fighters drink so much tea that their faces turn red. Father used *Filipendula*, I chose tamarisk.
>
> In its genre—it is a conversation of the poet in the tradition of V. Mayakovsky's "An Extraordinary Adventure ...:" inviting the sun, having a conversation with the sun, postulating the equivalence between the work of the sun and poet—to shine always and everywhere. ... In this way, Khoninov's text is not as simple as it appears: the themes are the sacred, history, the poet's role, etc."

One thing became immediately obvious on reading these words— Rimma was not happy with Kutov's translation. I saw my association of Khoninov's poem with Fet's (which virtually every child in Russia learns by heart) as an indicator of a light-hearted and positive attitude. Ironically, what she saw as childish, I saw as childlike, i.e. open, inviting, and sincere. My association of *WHY THE SUN IS RED* with Mayakovsky's poem arose primarily from the color and vibrancy of the images used in both. Only on second thought did I remember that Mayakovsky also had a poem about the sun.

Rimma's translation, on the other hand, lacked the playfulness that attracted me to Kutov's translation. It also did not trigger associations with Mayakovsky or Russian literature. It seemed to be a poem more attuned to the questions of history, ethnic identity, and philosophy of life. Since initially I thought that these were two different original poems, my assumption was that as life progressed the poet revisited some of the same themes from different perspectives and agendas. Realizing that the two Russian versions were actually one poem reinforced my belief that translating is a creative act that will inevitably reflect the personality and culture of the translator as much as, if not more than, the original words. It is remarkable that even though Rimma and the translator approached the poem from very different life and esthetic directions, we both arrived at all three themes of the poem: the dialogue of the poet and nature, the role of the poet in society, and the role of Kalmyk tea in Kalmyk history and identity. In light of that achievement, both translations must be deemed successful. This experience also shows the limits of purely formal analyses, or *Explication de Texte* (close reading), without contextual information when dealing with translated poetry. Without knowing that the two Russian translations were based on one Kalmyk text, all sorts of fanciful theories and explanations could have been built.

THE TEA BUSH

The first of Rimma Khaninova's poems about Kalmyk tea begins with a tale about the origin of tea. It recounts the legend of Bodhidharma cutting off his eyelids after he fell asleep during meditation. It is interesting that the poet writes about a legend that is popular in Japan, and not one that is Kalmyk, or even Chinese.

DZHOMBA

Footnotes as a device in poetry are not often encountered. Normally, footnotes are appended to translated, or old, poetry, where details of subject matter or context would not be obvious. In *DZHOMBA*, however, the original poem of some 40 lines is graced with 11 footnotes. In this poem footnotes allow the poet (who wrote in Russian) to use non-Russian terms and unfamiliar expressions without loss of meaning while maintaining meter and the desired sound values. They also help to underline the existence of at least two differing realities (Russian-Kalmyk) which are interconnected. Since the poet is also a noted scholar, the footnotes could serve as a playful reminder of the poetic and scholarly reality she inhabits. Lastly, the use of footnotes may also be carrying a gentle reminder that Kalmyk terms and folk forms are becoming exotic to a more Russified contemporary Kalmyk audience.

In translating the Russian version of the poem into English, the author's original format was not followed. This deliberate choice was motivated by the desire to ensure a smoother reading of the poem. Also, there was recognition that, to an English-language reader, the Russian and Kalmyk languages are equally exotic, and footnotes would serve few of the author's purposes. To ensure that the author's original work is included, her footnotes are listed here:

1. *ioral-* well-wish [poetic in form]
2. *arshan-* drink of the gods [ambrosia]
3. "Though tea is liquid, it's the first dish offered"—a Kalmyk saying
4. *Dzhomba*—the best Kalmyk tea Джомба.
5. "Has nothing to drink, but loves *dzhomba* [fine drinks]—Kalmyk proverb
6. *Aagh*—wooden tea bowl.
7. "Without will there is no strength, without salt there is no flavor"—Kalmyk saying.
8. "A wiry crone jumped up to the roof of the *ger* [yurt] (Ladle)"—Kalmyk riddle
9. "By the time you finish a cup of tea you will change ten times"—Kalmyk proverb stressing the leisure nature of tea drinking
10. Bumba—the promised land in the Kalmyk epic *Jangar*.
11. Jangar—the name of the epic hero and ruler.

The footnotes give the poem a scholarly cast and the poem can easily be approached as a poetic ethnography. The footnotes create a kind of Homeric catalog, which lists all the most important elements of spiritual and material culture that define the best Kalmyk tea—*dzhomba*. Most important, however, is the fact this poem was originally written in Russian and not Kalmyk, as was the case with the earlier poets. Rimma Khaninova, who was born in Siberia during the period of Kalmyk internal exile, and who grew up in a Russian school environment, marks the change from a generation who were unselfconsciously Kalmyk to one whose identity is both Kalmyk and Russian. Herein lies the tension between an inherited Kalmyk cultural practice and the expression of it in a language and culture that in the previous generations was largely foreign.

DZHOMBA is an ode written in praise of Kalmyk tea. Unlike Pushkin's "Monument" it does not use the two- or four-line stanzaic Horatian structure, but, seemingly with a wink towards it, the poem ends with an ellipsis and a four-line stanza. In mood and structure it is much closer to the heroic odes of Pindar and Russia's Gavrila Derzhavin (1743–1816) and his famous poem "Felicia."[47] The opening lines of the poem: *Godlike Princess/Of the Kirghiz-Kaisatsk Horde!* resonates with *DZHOMBA*'s: *Kalmyk tea ... lauded by the people/In proverbs, blessings, and in verse ...*

Derzhavin's poem was shamelessly flattering to Catherine II (for example, calling the 53-year old monarch a "princess") but rather scathing toward the courtiers that surrounded her. In that, his ode subverted the tradition of the genre which normally used high-flown rhetoric to praise heroic deeds. Rimma Khaninova's ode is not unflattering, but it does mix the "high" with the "low" and through use of irony creates a dramatic tension between the language and culture of the poem and the subject of it—tea. Using an ode, a genre associated with the 18th century in Russia, to sing the praises of tea today is verging on burlesque within that literary tradition. But from a Kalmyk perspective, where *dzhomba* was seen as a sacral food, such use of the ode would not appear amiss. Similarly, if we associate the poem with Derzhavin's "Felicia," then the lines:

---

[47] The original title of the poem was "Ode to the Wise Kirgiz-Princess Felitsa, Written by the Tartar Prince, Who Has Long-ago Settled in Moscow, But Who is Living in St. Petersburg For Business Reasons. Translated from the Arabic 1782."

> Tea in the bowl undulates, like a crone
> The ladle adroitly nestles on the edge
> Then bounds twixt cups, like nesting doll,
> Enthralling and enticing, as in the Promised Land.

also approach the burlesque. The juxtaposition of the everyday task of tea making and consumption with the heroic epic *Jangar*, once more calls to mind burlesque, but this time within a single culture.

One could easily go on with a more thorough analysis of this poem and show its connections to Pushkin and certain ideological positions set out by the poet, but poetic analysis is not the purpose of these commentaries—only setting out contexts and possibilities.

"It's often said …"

The opening line of this poem ("It's often said there's no disputing taste"), slightly restates the Russian proverb—"In color and taste there are no comrades;" Khaninova substitutes the traditional "comrades" with "friends." This perhaps is her most playful poem about Pushkin, and Carlton Copeland's translation captures her subtle irony well.

PUSHKIN'S TEXTS

The number of footnotes in *DZHOMBA* creates a scholarly feel to it. But *PUSHKIN'S TEXTS* could be called more scholarly if we consider that it uses verbatim references to Pushkin's *TO A KALMYK MAIDEN*, and also makes references to his diary and published journal. In essence, Khaninova's poem uses Pushkin's words to draw a critical portrait of his attitudes and behavior, and to laud the unknown Kalmyk woman who withstood his flirtatious attempts.

For the purposes of our work, the following specific points need to be noted. The first is the line: "Drank tea, alien to stomach and to soul." In this short line Khaninova establishes Pushkin's "foreignness," both in culinary terms and expected norms of behavior. The second point is found in the lines: "Pushkin's flirtation with the Kalmyk,/Could be a keepsake album poem." In these lines, Khaninova upends Pushkin's diary entry in which he writes that "he grew tired of Kalmyk flirtations." Khaninova realistically puts the onus of initiating the flirtation on the poet, not on the young woman. The argument is built that the stranger, either not knowing, or disregarding, Kalmyk norms of behavior created a situation that approaches the trivial or burlesque.

And lastly: "For the ephemeral buss/To that great-granny we are thankful ... / You did not forget honor and modesty." In these lines we clearly see Khaninova's argument that by adhering to the traditions of her culture the young Kalmyk woman not only preserved her own integrity but created a situation which, when transformed by Pushkin's poem and other writings, included the Kalmyks in Russian literary culture. The question is open, if a poem would have been written had Pushkin had his way, and had the young married Kalmyk woman, surrounded by her family, not defended herself against his advances. It is also obvious that Khaninova is not one of those who subscribe to the notion reported by Daniil Dolinskij in *A Place on Stage* that claim the young Kalmyk woman did not withstand Pushkin's challenge.

In this interpretation of the poem we see the manifestation of Borges' "Pierre Menard, Author of the Quixote." The poem is a very close restatement of Pushkin's *TO A KALMYK MAIDEN*, a mirror-image of sorts, which using his words addresses issues of contemporary concern such as the role of tradition and mores at points of juncture between cultures, and questions of gender/social parity. There are other layers inherent in this poem, but since they are not intrinsically connected to Kalmyk tea, they are best left for other commentary.

Quite some time was spent in a struggle to find the right place for this poem. At times the thought was to end the poetry section with it, thus providing a perfect frame—begin with Pushkin, end with Pushkin. That solution would be perfect in a work that focuses on Russian literature, but not in this book which is about tea, Kalmyk tea, and not about Russian literature.

TEA AND TEA BOWL

The poem, which concludes the book's poetry section, goes from the literary and historical to contemporary time. It is a *cri de couer* regarding Kalmyk tea, the passage of time and olden customs. This is one of the more directly personal poems written by Khaninova; there are no references to Japanese tea legends, to Pushkin, no listing of ethnographic or linguistic details. This poem is a meditation on loss; specifically, on the physical loss of a father's tea bowl. More generally, it is about social changes in which foreign and "innovative" objects replace the tried and true. The very oldest part of culture, like the wooden tea bowls, are preserved only in museums, but even more contemporary ceramic bowls are found wanting in today's world. Changes that go from the youth, and outside world, even affect the immediate family circle, leading the poet to wonder where this could end.

Ironically the poet charts her own participation in this process of change. First, she calls the old belief that drinking from a cracked cup brings ill fortune, "superstition"—a term of disdain or belittling. And she ends with the line that was translated as "Which century wafts outside?"[48] The Russian original mentions an outside yard, and indirectly indicates that the days of living in the *ger*, at one with nature, has been replaced with this concept of a yard, a term used by settled peoples who make a distinction between inside and outside. The world-view of the *ger*, which long served the Kalmyks as the symbol of the physical universe with the top ring circle of the tent denoting the border between the sentient universe and the world of the spirit—the blue sky (*tengri*), is gone today.

The enigmatic question of the last line could also be a reference to the time of internal exile when the Kalmyks, in clusters no larger than a family, were surrounded by strangers and strange ways. These strangers were the settled people whose dwellings had walls and yards. The poet and her family have since also become one with the stranger's world.

---

[48] Literally the line translates: "Which of the centuries is outside in the yard?"

Tea Bowl *(Aagh)*, 2014
(Photo N. Burlakoff)

EDITOR AND CONTRIBUTORS

EDITOR

Nikolai Burlakoff

Writer, editor, translator, photographer, and publisher. His most recent book, *The World of Russian Borsch* (2013), has had a positive response from historians of Russian cuisine. *Dzhomba* follows a successful collaboration with Rimma Khaninova and members of an international team that resulted in the well-received *A Kalmyk Sampler: Mongol Poetry and Mythic Tale* (2012). His fieldwork observations and research about Kalmyks are presented in *Steppe Notes*, numbers 1-19, available @ http://www.njfolkfest.rutgers.edu/2011_steppe1.html. He is currently working on a book about Russian Buddhism.

CONTRIBUTORS

Tamara Goyaevna Basangova (Bordzhanova)

Was born in Siberia. She began her studies at the Kalmyk State University and completed her doctoral work at the Institute of Eastern Studies of the Academy of Sciences. Her dissertation, *The Problems of Poetics in the Mongolo-Oirat Heroic Epos*, was successfully defended in 1975. Since 1976 she has worked as a researcher at the Kalmyk Research Institute of Language, History, and Literature currently affiliated with the Russian Academy of Sciences. She has been a member of numerous folklore fieldwork projects and is constantly in demand at international, national, and regional conferences and symposia.

Her published books include: *Kalmyk Tercets* (1987), «Сагла ээжин туульс» (1989), *Kalmyk Folklore: A Bibliographic Index* (1991), *The Magic Poetry of the Kalmyk: Research and Materials* (1999), *The Sandalwood Chest: Kalmyk Folktales* (2002), *Ritual Poetry of Kalmyks (System of Genres and Poetics)* (2007), *Kalmyk Children's Folklore* (2009), *The Typology of Kalmyk Folklore* (2014).

Her work has earned her recognition as an honored scholar of the Republic of Kalmykia.

Gail S. Burlakoff
Gail Shaw Burlakoff, editor and poet, has been a professional editor for more than 30 years. With a love of and facility with languages, she approaches editing as a sort of translation. Her chapbook, *Blue Heron Woman: Poems,* was published by AElitaPress.org in 2014.

Vasilii Bairovich Chongonov
Native of Kalmykia. Poet, translator, chairman of "Zokyalch"—the Center for Translation and Propagation of Kalmyk Literature, and consultant to the regional department of the Writers Union of Kalmykia.

Carleton Copeland
Translator. A native of Detroit, Carleton Copeland fell in love with the Russian language at the University of Michigan. Pursuing his passion to Leningrad in the 1980s, he spent several delirious winters living in ramshackle dormitories, muttering verb conjugations, and wandering the streets of the crumbling imperial capital. The charm has never worn off. He now works as a translator for Ernst & Young in Moscow and spends many evenings and weekends obsessively translating Russian poetry.

Erdni Antonovich Eldyshev
Poet and translator. Graduate of the Kalmyk State University. Member of the Russian Union of Writers. Chair of the governing body of the Kalmyk Union of Writers. National Poet of Kalmykia. Laureate of Literary Awards.

The author of books of poetry: *Native Hearth, Morning Flight, Seven Cranes, Grandpa's Pipe,* and others.

Elzabair Guchinova
Social anthropologist, Doctor of Historical Sciences. An associate of the European University in St. Peterburg. The author of four monographs about Kalmyk identity. Grant recipient of the MacArthur Foundation, Fulbright, Alexander von Humboldt , the Japanese Foundation, and others. In recent years her major focus has been the study of past traumas and its reflection in narratives (language and art).

Rimma Khaninova
Poet, playwright, and translator. Graduate of the Kalmyk State University. Holder of a PhD in Philological Studies. Head of the Department of Russian and Foreign Literatures. Writes in Russian. Member of the Russian Union of Writers. Author of poetry and narrative poem collections: *Winter Rain* (1993), *Soaring Over Worldly Bustle* (1994), *Smart*

Mouse (2002), *The Letter "A"* (2010). She also co-authored, with Mikhail Khaninov, *The Hour of Speech* (2002), *I'll Become a Red Tulip* (2010) and, with Ilya Nichiporov, *At the Crossroads of Sophia and Faith* (2005).

She is the author of four monographs about Russian and Kalmyk literature. The daughter of the well-known Kalmyk poet Mikhail Khoninov (1919-1981), she is the publisher of his literary legacy. Her personal web site is: www. ханинова.рф

Mikhail Khoninov

He was born in 1919 in the Kalmyk village, Tsagan Nur, in the Astrakhan Province, and died in 1981. Khoninov was a veteran of the Smolensk Campaign, after the German attack on the Soviet Union, and he became a famed guerilla leader in Byelorussia. For his military exploits he was awarded the Order of the Red Banner, and for his cultural accomplishments he was awarded the People's Friendship Medal. Despite his service in WWII he was exiled, with other Kalmyks, to Siberia.

Khoninov was an actor, the first director of the Kalmyk radio station, a playwright, prose and poetry writer, and translator.

He published 36 books of prose and poetry, including two children's books, with many of his works becoming translated.

Nikolai Nikolaevich Kutov (1917-1998)

Poet and translator. Member of the Writers Union since 1950, he worked for many years in the magazine *Zvezda* [Star]. His translations include poems from Byelorussian, Uigur, Mari, Kazakh, Kalmyk, Tyva, Mordovian Komi, and Kabardian.

David Nikitich Kutulganov (1922-2006)

Published his first poem at age 12 and became a member of the Writers Union at 18. In 1941 he went to fight in WWII, and in 1944 he was deported to the Altai Region in Siberia. He spent the bulk of his 15-year exile in Norilsk. In 1957 he returned to Kalmykia. He completed his literary studies as a correspondence student at the Gorky Literary Institute.. The Kalmyk national epic poem *Djangar* provided a major influence on his writing.

He was the author of many poems, the narrative poem *The Rebellion of Reason*, and poetic fairy tales.

Walter C. May

Walter C. May was born on December 22, 1912, in Britain. He died in Moscow in 2005. In the 1960s he met, in Moscow, his second wife, the poet and prose writer Lyudmilla Grigorievna Serostanova (Lucy), born in Dagestan. Since 1967 he had been living in Moscow. or its former suburb Scherbinka. He is a translator of Pushkin's poems and a host of other classical and modern poets, including Akhmadulina. He took great interest in epic poetry and translated the Russian *Song of Igor's Campaign*, the Ossetian *The Tales of Narts* (Heroes), and the Kyrgyz *Manas*. In June of 2013 his wife published *Meridian of Love*, a bilingual collection of poetry she had co-authored with Walter.

Avril Pyman (aka Dr. Avril Sokolov FBA)

Writer, translator, researcher, lecturer and reader at University of Durham. Studied in Leningrad, freelancer in Moscow.

Books and Publications

As Avril Pyman: *Life of Aleksander Blok vol 1: The Distant Thunder* (1979), *Life of Aleksander Blok vol 2: The Release of Harmony* (1980), *History of Russian Symbolism* (1994), *Anna Akhmatova, Requiem* (trans with engravings by K Sokolov, 2003), *Fedor Tiutchev, A Selection of Poems* (trans with engravings by K Sokolov, 2003), *Pavel Florensky, a Quiet Genius* (2010).

Vera Kirguevna Shugraeva

Kalmyk National Poet, writer, journalist, teacher, playwright, translator, song writer, librettist, screen writer. The author of thirty books. Received in 2006 from the Orthodox Patriarch of Russia the medal of St. Innocent, the Metropolitan of Moscow, for her translation of the Psalter from Russian to Kalmyk. In 2011, she received the Chekov medal for her contributions to contemporary Russian literature.